SUPPORTING

STRUGGLING

LEARNERS

SUPPORTING

STRUGGLING

LEARNERS

50 Instructional Moves for the Classroom Teacher

Heinemann

DEDICATED TO TEACHERS™

PATRICIA VITALE-REILLY

Heinemann

361 Hanover Street

Portsmouth, NH 03801–3912

www.heinemann.com

Offices and agents throughout the world

Library of Congress Cataloging-in-Publication Data

Names: Vitale-Reilly, Patricia, author.

Title: Supporting struggling learners : 50 instructional moves for the classroom teacher / Patricia Vitale-Reilly.

Description: Portsmouth, NH : Heinemann, [2017]

Identifiers: LCCN 2017020661 | ISBN 9780325088785

Subjects: LCSH: Remedial teaching.

Classification: LCC LB1029.R4 V57 2017 | DDC 371.102—dc23

LC record available at https://lccn.loc.gov/2017020661

Acquisitions Editor: Holly Kim Price

Production Editor: Sean Moreau

Cover Design: Suzanne Heiser

Interior Design: Valerie Levy, Drawing Board Studios

Typesetter: Valerie Levy, Drawing Board Studios

Manufacturing: Steve Bernier

Printed in the United States of America on acid-free paper

21 20 19 18 17 PAH 1 2 3 4 5

This book is dedicated to Patricia Hoy—
my mother, my first teacher, my mentor, my friend.

Contents

Supporting Struggling Learners Online Resources

To access the online resources for *Supporting Struggling Learners*, please go to www.heinemann.com and click the link in the upper right to **Log In.**

(If you do not already have an account with Heinemann, you will need to create an account.)

Register your product by entering the code: **SSLEARNERS.**

Once you have registered your product, it will appear in the list of **My Online Resources.**

Acknowledgments

I am so happy to have this book out in the world, having been writing it on and off for over five years and working on the ideas it contains for many decades. I am deeply grateful to all of the educators who have inspired me, pushed my thinking, and allowed me into their classrooms, offices, and schools. In doing so they have had such a positive and profound impact on this book. In particular, my deepest thanks to:

Meaghan Arias, Diane Baker, Susan Cooper, Marissa DePalma, Jean DeSimone, Anthony DiNoto, Tammy Ficarelli, Talysa Glogower, Janine Grosso, Lisa Horst, Alisa Kadus, Mary Mark, Amanda Melican, Erin Murphy, Betsy Peterson, Jody Skidd, and Crystal Tuozzolo.

I would also like to thank the following schools and districts for our professional collaborations:

The Cathedral School of Saint John the Divine, Emerson Public Schools, Fort Lee Public Schools, Nyack Public Schools, Princeton Day School, Saddle River Day School, and the Warwick Valley Public School System.

A big thank you to my colleagues and friends who support me in so many ways, big and small: Lindsay Agar, Lisa Eickholdt, Bev Gallagher, Jaime Margolies, Marybeth O'Connor, Sally Rubin-Richards, and Elena Skinner.

Many thanks to my editor, Holly Kim Price, for believing in this book, supporting my thinking, answering all of my questions, and shaping my ideas. Thanks to the amazing Heinemann team of Steve Bernier, Amanda Bondi, Suzanne Heiser, Pam Hunt, Valerie Levy, Sean Moreau, Jane Orr, and Elizabeth Silvis who make this process as seamless as possible and for supporting this book from idea, to draft, to edits, to design, and to production.

And most especially, I thank my family — Kevin, Rhiannon, and Jack Reilly. Thank you for always believing in my work, for giving me time at my desk and knowing when to pull me away from it, and for your love and support, always.

Introduction

As teachers, our days are filled with many things—everyday minutia, grand successes, endless mandates, and joyous small moments. And in those full days, we live alongside our students . . . ALL of them. Some students live in our minds easily. They are growing, they are happy, learning is going smoothly for them. Yet for other students, learning is not going so smoothly. They are not happy and not growing in the ways we want them to.

These students are always on our minds. We take them home with us and think about them at odd moments. I was young when I began teaching, barely a decade older than the students I taught, and that first year together was part trial by fire, part camp counselor, part experiment. During that year, it was Stephen who occupied my thoughts and plagued me with worry.

> *Is he learning?*
>
> *Is he happy?*
>
> *Is my classroom the right place for him?*
>
> *Am I doing what I need to be doing to help him achieve*
> *his goals as a learner?*
>
> *Is there something else I could be doing?*

Stephen was, on many fronts, a struggling learner. He had an attention deficit hyperactivity disorder diagnosis, coupled with some mild processing and anxiety issues. He struggled to organize his thinking in writing, which affected not only reading and writing but social studies and science as well. He had trouble with handwriting, so he struggled to get his ideas down in legible ways. He had some social difficulties, too, and had trouble connecting with the other boys in the class. Many times at the beginning of the year, he came back from recess angry or upset. Once, he actually left the playground during recess and came up to my classroom to spend recess with me instead of playing with his classmates. He couldn't quite understand why the other students wouldn't play his version of dodge ball or why he should try to work out conflicts.

Stephen was also one of the most curious and creative learners I have ever met. His capacity for understanding texts and his interpretations of characters, events, and themes was unparalleled. When I realized that Stephen could not sit in our meeting area for lessons and for read-aloud, I let him do laps in the back of the classroom. Yet the thinking he shared about either the lesson or the text was always right on and insightful, bringing our work to another level.

Stephen was just the first. There were Anna and Tomeo, Michael and Odin, Amy and Malachi, Stephanie and James and . . . you see what I mean. As you are reading this, your own list of names might be running through your head.

As Stephen's teacher, I was plagued with questions. And I knew that for him, and for myself, I needed to find answers. So I took this on, really on, as an inquiry into my personal professional development, and discovered things that have shaped my beliefs about how struggling learners learn best.

Many times, we think of struggling learners based on a deficit model. When I was teaching Stephen, I constantly worried about supporting him as a learner. Could I help him harness his thoughts in a coherent way? Would I be able to find a reading and writing partner with whom he could work? What about all of the materials I was introducing him to? Would he be able to use these? And what about when he got to the middle school—what would happen then?

I understand that we teachers are "fixers," and finding what is getting in a student's way will help us determine what he needs. However, let's not allow this idea to frame how we support struggling learners. Instead, let's use what positive psychology has taught us about student success: Every student has strengths—whether resources, talents, skills, or motivations—and those strengths should be the pillar on which we stand (Anderson 2005). We don't ignore the deficits but capitalize on the strengths (Clifton, Anderson, and Schreiner 2016) so we can design teaching moves, including specific interventions, that are grounded in what students can do well to propel them forward.

Tomlinson (2014) reminds us that learners are different. In turn, our classrooms must be laboratories where differentiated learning can exist.

> Thus, teachers in differentiated classrooms accept and act on the premise that they must be ready to engage students in instruction through different approaches to learning, by appealing to a range of interests, and by using varied rates of instruction along with varied degrees of complexity and different support systems. In differentiated classrooms, teachers ensure that students compete against themselves as they grow and develop more than they compete against one another, always moving toward—and often beyond—designated content goals.
>
> In other words, teachers who differentiate provide specific alternatives for individuals to learn as deeply as possible and as quickly

as possible, without assuming one student's road map for learning is
identical to anyone else's. (3–4)

I started off big. I thought about different curricula, different placements for Stephen
and others, and drastically different approaches. I had my heart in the right place,
but those big changes weren't working. Stephen certainly was not going to learn to
handle collaborations positively if he was isolated from his peers. As I got to know
Stephen, I began to realize what a critical thinker he was. He did not need any modifications to the curriculum; he needed me to accommodate him and his learning to
match his challenges. I realized that small changes—instructional moves geared to
what the learner needs most in that moment—implemented inside my classroom,
alongside our learning and learners, could make a big difference.

What You Will Find in This Book

The classroom environment can either support or impede learners, so in Chapter 1,
I propose small instructional moves that you can make to enable learners to access
ideas and learning.

I learned that peer support helps all learners, especially those who struggle. In
Chapter 2 I tackle peer learning—learning centers and group projects—and suggest
ways to use everyday structures to support our struggling learners.

Many students are visual learners, so in Chapter 3 I lay out simple ways to use
visuals in instruction and practice for both teaching and learning.

One of the ways I supported Stephen and other struggling learners was with pre-
teaching. Pre-teaching can feel hard to implement. We wonder: When will I have
time to pre-teach? How will I pre-teach? Whom will I pre-teach and why? In Chapter
4, I offer easy yet powerful pre-teaching strategies.

One of the most profound ways I have been able to support struggling learners is through small-group instruction in reading, writing, math, and content areas.
Chapter 5, which tackles small-group instruction, is chock full of samples of small-
group instruction, classroom examples, and planners and other record-keeping tools.

Building certain academic and life skills can benefit students who struggle, so I
devoted Chapters 6 and 7 to study skills and communication skills, respectively.

Another place where we can implement instructional moves that have huge benefits is to support all students as writers. Writing is a discipline that stands alone, yet
it travels with us across the day and across other disciplines. Providing students with
specific writing strategies—planning, brainstorming, and organization—can help
them be successful learners. Chapter 8 tackles writing across the day and includes
effective strategies for our struggling students.

Chapter 9 embraces the idea that strong home-school connections support every learner. In this chapter I share my thinking around collaboration and communication as a wrap-around approach to supporting students who struggle.

Chapter 10 offers my final thoughts and suggestions organized in an *If/Then* structure. If a student needs more support; if you need to progress-monitor a student; if you have a co-teacher, specialist, or an instructional aide in your room with you; if your teaching is not sticking, then take a look at my go-to list of tried and true solutions, which include instructional approaches, accommodations, tools, and protocols.

Why This Book for Classroom Teachers?

I have been thinking of writing a book about struggling learners for many years and for many reasons. I'm sure a tiny seed was planted even when I was a young child, and that seed began to grow as soon as I started working with children and young adults. We will (unfortunately) always have students in our classrooms who struggle. They struggle in many different ways—different in both the reasons why they struggle and the ways in which they struggle. Since each and every classroom will have struggling learners, it is helpful to define the kinds of struggling learners we might encounter in our classrooms and then plan moves to support them.

Who Are Struggling Learners?

The term "struggling learners" is a widely used and incredibly broad term. When teachers and schools use the term, they do so to describe special education students mandated to receive services, students identified as struggling learners who receive mandated or nonmandated supplemental academic intervention services, and other students who receive no additional support or services as well. Let's look carefully at what I see as the three cohorts of struggling learners.

SPECIAL EDUCATION STUDENTS

Students who qualify for special education services are struggling learners. These students have been classified as students who are to mandated to receive special education services, delivered by a certified special education teacher. The laws governing these mandates are most recently through IDEA, the Individuals with Disabilities Education Improvement Act of 2004. According to this legislation, special education is defined as "specially designed instruction, at no cost to the parents, to meet the unique needs of a child with a disability."

To deliver specially designed instruction that will meet the unique needs of a child with a disability, it is important to determine not only the learner's disability but, more importantly, the learner's strengths and what the learner struggles with. For example, a student may have a classification of "Specific Learning Disability," which according to IDEA (1997) is defined as "a disorder in one or more of the basic psychological processes involved in understanding or in using language, spoken or written, that may manifest itself in the imperfect ability to listen, think, speak, read, write, spell, or to do mathematical calculations. The term includes such conditions as perceptual disabilities, brain injury, minimal brain dysfunction, dyslexia, auditory processing disorders and developmental aphasia."

This broad statement, meant to describe the classification of "Specific Learning Disability," is helpful in determining what classification the student will receive and, in turn, can determine pertinent services. Yet to develop specific techniques and strategies that will most effectively teach this student, it is essential to determine *what* specifically the student struggles with. Does this learner struggle with reading? If so, with what aspects of reading—decoding? Inferring a main or central idea? Responding to reading? Does the learner struggle with math? If so, with what aspects of math—remembering math facts and equations? Applying the correct mathematical equation to solve the problem? Understanding multistep word problems? All of the above? Identifying the specific struggles of special education students is essential for creating the most effective instructional moves you will implement for this learner.

STUDENTS DESIGNATED TO RECEIVE MANDATED OR NONMANDATED SUPPLEMENTAL INSTRUCTION

Struggling learners are also those students who have been identified as needing additional support. These students are typically designated to receive support in a variety of subjects through programs titled "basic skills instruction" or "academic intervention services." These are the students in our classrooms who do not meet the requisite benchmarks we have put forth for our students, including yearly standardized tests, local diagnostic and formative assessments, and other school-based metrics. Students who receive supplemental instruction usually do not meet the above-mentioned metrics in reading and math and therefore are given additional support.

Marie Clay, innovative educator and founder of Reading Recovery has stated that, "70 percent of students will learn to read without struggle." Approximately 10 percent of our population is identified as learning disabled. This leaves somewhere around 20 percent of our students who are typically—and, more importantly, should be—identified in this cohort of struggling learners: learners who need supplemental instruction.

INTERMITTENT STRUGGLERS

This last category of struggling learner is not as easy to define. These students are not mandated for special education services and typically do not fall into the cohort of students who receive ongoing, systematic supplemental support. Yet they—and potentially any student—can struggle at any time in their school career.

These struggles may be related to an incident or event in a student's life, such as a home, personal, or social situation, that causes the learner to struggle and interferes with the typical progress he or she might make.

Other times, the struggle is contextual: There is a topic, course, or specific learning context that is challenging for the student. This is not to say the struggle is not real; it is just contextualized around a topic, moment of learning, or context that amplifies a weakness in the student's memory, organization, time management, or other skills.

Sometimes, students just occasionally struggle. We have all had them in our classrooms; you know who they are. They are always on our radar, our "watch list," but we know they will never qualify for services and do not need special education or supplemental services. They do, however, need instruction and support that intervenes in their learning and enables them to get past the struggle.

I have been thinking about struggling students for decades. You see, my journey didn't start with Stephen. It started with Tommy. In September 1968, two parents meet with the elementary school principal. Their son, Tommy, has a learning disability, yet no one is quite clear what it is. Although Tommy's parents are unclear of what he needs or what is getting in the way, Tommy is already struggling in school. During kindergarten, he has trouble following directions, and emergent literacy skills (such as learning letters, sounds, and how books work) are a challenge for him. Tommy's parents want to investigate the options for him. The principal leads them down a set of stairs to the basement. There, next to the boiler, is a room for children who are "different."

One child is in a wheelchair. He appears to be a capable student academically but is physically handicapped. Next to him are two students with Down syndrome. Across the room is a child who is there for behavioral concerns. He is identified by the teacher as a child who is a "lot of trouble" for his teachers.

Tommy's parents aren't sure why they are being shown this classroom. The learners are all quite different. In addition, Tommy, like all children, possesses many strengths. He is the fifth child in his family, and having lived with four older siblings, all close in age, and a large extended family, he is quite verbal. His expressive language skills are age appropriate, including his articulation and content, and he is able to hold interesting conversations with both peers and adults. He is also a curious learner with a great imagination. Tommy spends long afternoons in his backyard and in the accompanying woods playing many a game of make-believe and learning to play sportslike games such as Red Rover, kickball, and manhunt. He has age-appropriate gross and fine motor skills and enjoys group games and board games of all kinds. In addition, Tommy has an incredible memory. He can remember dates and experiences far beyond what a child of his age typically can.

His strengths are not a part of the conversation, or even part of the decision-making used to inform Tommy's placement or education. Tommy's parents ask the principal what Tommy's other options are. The principal looks at them, confused. He says, "There are no other options. It is here in this room, or in one of the first-grade classrooms."

Tommy went on to one of the first-grade classrooms and struggled for many years in school.

You see, Tommy is actually my brother. In the 1970s, I did a lot of learning along-side him. I learned what he was learning, and even though he is six years my senior, I took it upon myself to teach him what he needed to learn. This experience forever shaped me and led me to a career in education.

At the end of the day, they are *all* our students, and I think sometimes we forget that. We want so much for Tommy and Stephen to be successful that we think we can find a place, a program, or a person who can help them. And those things may indeed help our struggling students in some way, but as classroom teachers, we can implement moves and make a difference in our students' learning and in their lives. All we need to do is make some small changes.

CHAPTER ONE

Create an Inclusive Culture Through Structures and Environment

Last year I went to my son's middle school to meet with his English language arts (ELA) teacher. As I entered Susan Cooper's sixth-grade ELA room, I immediately felt that this was a room in which he could learn. There were many tangible elements I could point to: the seats were arranged in collaborative structures, technology was available and clearly a part of the fabric of the classroom, and evidence of teaching and learning existed in the environment through anchor charts and student work. However, many elements were much harder to identify. This room, which exuded the feeling of a place that welcomed and embraced all students, represented what I like to call an inclusive culture.

I define culture as the tone of the room—both the tangible and the intangible vibe, ethos, or spirit of a community of learners. Building an inclusive culture means that you create a space—both physical and social-emotional—that not only welcomes each student but also works for each student. The room fits them and their needs.

Research supports this. The universal design for learning (typically referred to as UDL) initiative was first defined by Harvard educator David H. Rose (1998) but was originally an architectural design framework called universal design. It informed and influenced the way architects designed buildings to be inclusive of all individuals (Story, Mace, and Mueller 1998). This included building ramps at the entrance of buildings, incorporating automatic doors, and using voice technology in elevators. What they discovered was that many people benefitted from this inclusive design. As Conn-Powers, Cross, Traub, and Hutter-Pishgahi (2006) explain in "The Universal Design of Early Education: Moving Forward for All Children,"

> At first these design applications may seem solely intended for people with disabilities. But developers of the universal design framework

1

recognized that usability would increase as special needs features began to serve all. People who use wheelchairs benefit from curb cuts and ramps, but so do bicycle riders, parents pushing strollers, and travelers pulling wheeled luggage. Elevators that announce floor numbers assist individuals with impaired sight along with shorter people who may not be able to see the light indicators when the elevator is crowded with riders. Doors that open automatically aid those not strong enough to open them as well as individuals whose arms hold packages or young children.

After becoming aware of universal design, the field of education took on the idea of incorporating its seven principles into the fabric of our classrooms. In particular, the principle of "size and space for appropriate use" translated into the idea of recreating spaces to be inclusive of all students.

Considering how to create the most appropriate and useful environment for learning is essential. In "Instructional Theories Supporting Universal Design for Learning—Teaching to Individual Learners," Mason, Orkwis, and Scott claim "Classroom environment and the organization of curricular materials allow for variations in physical and cognitive access by students as well as for variations in instructional methods; classroom environment allows for varied student groupings; classroom space encourages learning" (2005).

The first moves you can make to support struggling learners will enable you to create a learning environment that is conducive for all students. And although tone and culture can sometimes seem intangible, we can make tangible moves to create an inclusive culture that will enable our struggling students to thrive.

 ## #1 *Make Your Room and Walls Clutter Free (K–8)*

This concept is simple yet profound. My belief in creating an uncluttered, visually supportive environment that would not overstimulate students started many years ago when I first began teaching. I taught in a Waldorf school, an the Waldorf pedagogy closely matches the UDL principle that design should be "simple and intuitive." This means that we do not overcomplicate our environment and fill it with every imaginable tool, thought, material, and decoration. We carefully curate our materials and have students interact with them in simple and intuitive ways.

I believe the classroom environment can be considered an additional teacher, so begin with the materials. Students do need a variety of materials for learning, but we do not need to present all the materials to our students, all of the

Figure 1.1a: Lisa Horst's Grade 3 Writing Center

time. Figure 1.1a shows how classroom materials can be organized and clutter-free. Rotate materials as they are needed throughout the year. This can include materials for labs and science experiments, manipulatives for math, and even books for our classroom libraries. I am a book junkie and this one took me a long time to embrace, but having such a busy library can challenge many of our students. Add and subtract books as the year goes on, perhaps adding books of increasing complexity for primary or middle elementary students, or adding genres, subjects, and themes as they become pertinent across the year for upper-elementary and middle school students. You might even consider splitting up the library. For example, keep multiple sets of books (text pairs, certain genres or themes, or book club selections) in another section of the room. This will allow students to access different types of materials in different spaces—a much easier task to manage. Figures 1.1b, 1.1c, and 1.1d show how second–grade teacher Anthony DiNoto has multiple sections to his classroom library. Classrooms are crowded, and removing materials from the room creates a better flow and an increased chance for access and independent use of materials.

This principle applies to our walls as well. I often encourage teachers to think about how the wall space is used up. Consider removing any store-bought or premade visuals—they may not feel relevant to our students and frequently distract them. Do not hang every anchor chart from every discipline on your

Figure 1.1b–1.1d: Anthony DiNoto's Grade 2 Library Center

walls at all times. For struggling students, visual stimulation actually impedes learning. If possible, consider the color choice of walls and materials, and use warm, soft, and/or muted hues instead of bright, loud colors. Chapter 3 provides more moves that address the use of visuals in the environment, especially the use of anchor charts.

#2 Offer Multiple, Flexible Seating Arrangements (K–5)

Students spend many hours in school, sometimes more than they spend awake at home, so it is important to keep the environment in which they learn functional and comfortable. Unfortunately, many of our schools still have traditional environments that do not work for many of our students. Although altering the architecture and layout of our classrooms might be difficult, changing seating options is one move that we can make to support all of our learners.

During the course of a day, students should be allowed to sit on chairs of different sizes, styles, and heights, on the floor, leaning on a secure surface (such as the wall), or on special seats (such as balls or seats designed to support posture and focus). Where a student sits should be his choice and should be part of the early discussions that you have with students regarding where and how they will work in your classroom. Once these conversations occur, students can sit in that "seat" for a predetermined amount of time until seating options can be changed—for the day, for the week, or even for the unit of study if that makes the most sense.

Where students sit can impact how they learn, so it is important to recognize that this seemingly innocuous element can affect student success. For some students, sitting in a typical school chair for an entire day can actually be torturous. So too can sitting on the floor unsupported. Young learners who have postural weaknesses (in simple terms, weak core muscles and control), sitting on the floor unsupported actually taxes their body, and attention, focus, and understanding are compromised. Therefore, it is important to provide multiple seating options for various times of the day. For example, when I gathered my students in a central

Figure 1.2: Standing Desk

area for a minilesson or class meeting, they could sit on the carpet unsupported or leaning on the wall, on a chair (that they brought to the meeting area), or on the floor on a supportive seat (sometimes called a wiggle cushion). They even had the option to stand. My fourth-grade student Stephen would stand for the entire read-aloud, sometimes in one place, but frequently lapping the back of the classroom. Now there are standing desks, some with a movable bar below that students can pedal while working, that work very well for struggling learners. Figure 1.2 shows an example of a standing desk with a pedal. In fact, you can now purchase an inexpensive, stretchable band, called Bouncy Bands (www.bouncy bands.com), that can be attached to any chair or desk to allow students to bounce and stretch their legs.

Figures 1.3a–1.3c: Flexible Seating

Having varied workspace options is also important. Teachers frequently ask my thoughts regarding desks and tables and where students should sit during independent practice. My answer is: anywhere and everywhere. Regardless of the discipline, my students could be found in every available space in the classroom. This includes on the floor (on their bottom, a seat, or even on their stomachs, leaning on a clipboard), on one of the comfortable nontraditional seating options (large pillows, rocking chairs, and so on), at a desk (I always had a few of those in my room), or at a table (I had a few, in various places, of different heights, sizes and shapes). I called where they chose to work their "smart spot," and I put a lot of stock into thinking carefully about seating arrangements and how I could support my struggling students by providing them comfortable options. I even offered my desk as an option. As the years went by, I realized that I did not want a traditional teacher's desk placed front and center in my classroom. I gradually reduced the size of the desk until it was the smallest desk we had in our building (slightly larger than a typical student desk, but wooden, with drawers), and I put my desk in a corner facing a board or wall. This actually became a great option for students who needed a little help "tuning out" the working hum and visual stimulation of the room, and I shared this seating with many a struggling student over the years. Figures 1.3a, 1.3b, and 1.3c show a classroom with multiple, flexible seating arrangements.

#3   *Present Information in Multiple Media (K–8)*

Learners are different, and as such, they will process information differently. Although we want our classrooms to be active, student-centered environments, sometimes we will need to present information to our students. Therefore, when we are in minilesson mode, we want to make sure that we have multiple media for teaching and learning, not just presenting information orally. This move to presenting learning in multiple media stands on the shoulders of one of the three UDL principles defined by the Center for Applied Special Technology—incorporating multiple means of representation (Mason, Orkwis, and Scott 2005). When we impart knowledge to our students by demonstrating, using a model, or instructing, we provide an additional medium through which students receive and process the information.

This is about more than providing visuals, although that is always a great start. In Chapter 3 I unpack the moves around using visuals in teaching. Here, I am also talking about providing students with physical, tactile, and kinesthetic materials and opportunities to learn.

For minilessons that involve texts, have extra copies of these texts available for student use. Sometimes, all students might have a text, or the text is visually displayed during reading, as in the case of a shared or close read. However, during read-aloud, the teacher is typically the only reader with a copy of the text. Be sure to have extra copies of read-aloud texts (especially chapter books for middle- and upper-grade students) so students can follow along. For certain struggling learners, this move provides the visual support they need to engage with and understand the text.

We understand the impact of success criteria on student achievement (Hattie 2009), so we want to incorporate rubrics and checklists as often and as clearly as possible. Therefore, when contemplating multiple means of representation, consider incorporating a visual rubric in your writing center (or area of the classroom designated to writing). A visual rubric demonstrates the differences between a 1, 2, 3, and 4 in writing, using a teacher-created example. Figure 1.4 shows an example of a visual rubric.

When teaching math, keep manipulatives within students' reach. I had a variety of math materials in small caddies on tables and surfaces during the minilesson. Sometimes, all students used the materials, but other times, they were available for individual use. For example, Tammy could be using the base-ten blocks on a mat during our place-value lesson, while Phillip could be using the fraction circle during a lesson on fractions and decimals. And the same was true of science materials during science lessons. I gave students time at the beginning of the year to get to know the manipulatives/tools and to "play" with the materials. After that they were able to use them well, at appropriate times, and with intention.

I am a firm believer in the power of kinesthetic movement for learning, especially for struggling learners. Why? For them, understanding multiple parts to a story, multiple steps to a process, and remembering the multiple steps necessary to complete a task (whether in a text to be read or written, a historical event, a math problem, or a series of directions) can be challenging because of weak working memory. What is working memory? It is a part of the short-term memory system that takes in visual and auditory input and processes and stores the input in the short term. Information does not go into long-term memory until it is processed in our working memory.

Research on ways to support students with weak working memory supports the notion that it is best to use strategies that decrease working memory stress and overload, rather than try to improve working memory. How can we decrease working memory overload without decreasing the expectations we have for students? We can chunk information and provide students with tangible ways to process this information in the short term. One way I do that is to add kinesthetic movement to the processing procedure. For example, I allow students to add physical movement to reading and writing when they are interacting

I went to the beach with my family.

I went to the beach with my family. We went swimming and played in the waves.

I went to the beach with my family. It was a warm and sunny day. We went swimming and played in the waves.

I went to the beach with my family. It was a warm and sunny day. We went swimming and played in the waves. I said to my brother, "Swimming is fun!"

Figure 1.4: Visual Writing Rubric

with texts. In reading, you might add movement to retellings, or even allow them to act out a sequence of events, a problem or solution a character had, or even a reaction or motivation to the problem. In writing, you might allow students to touch the page while planning their writing, literally adding the tapping movement while stating the parts to the text. In math, I incorporate kinesthetic movement while teaching division. Although I have a variety of algorithms and "tricks" for both completing equations and understanding the concept, I find that the movement around the basic steps really supports learners who are struggling with the concept. For those of you who know the jazz "step ball change" move, it is a variation of that to the words: "divide, multiply, subtract, get the remainder." Chunking the steps of division—divide, multiply, subtract, get the remainder—and putting those steps to song and dance decreases working memory demands and enables learners to process and use the steps necessary for solving the equation. In *Math on the Move*, Malke Rosenfeld writes, "when children harness their innate body knowledge for mathematical sense making, they also harness their whole selves in the pursuit of new ideas and understanding" (2017). Adding kinesthetic movement is quite effective (and fun)!

#4 *Allow Students to Show Understanding in Multiple Forms (K–8)*

Allowing students to show understanding in multiple forms also plays off of one of the three UDL principles—incorporating multiple means of expression. For a variety of reasons, expressing understanding is hard for many struggling learners. Sometimes, a learner has trouble putting thoughts to words and is unclear of what he or she wants to say. Other times, the learner knows what he or she wants to say but has trouble expressing it clearly and succinctly. And in other cases, a learner is taking time to process input and just needs time to express understanding. Regardless, we serve all our learners well when we provide students with multiple ways to demonstrate understanding. Examples are shown below in Figure 1.5.

ROLE PLAY	Demonstrate scientific conclusions (such as the movement of molecules or the change in rock formations), plot elements or character change in a text, or depict an event of historical significance through a short skit or even pantomime. Role playing can happen individually, in pairs, or in small groups.

Figure 1.5: Multiple Means of Expressing Understanding   *(continues)*

Figure 1.5   *(continued)*

VERBAL EXPRESSION WITH CONFIRMATION	When a student expresses thinking, an opinion, or understanding, offer verbal confirmation. One way to offer verbal confirmation is to state back to students what you heard: "So what I believe I hear you saying is . . ." This helps acknowledge students' thinking (I never stray far from their original thoughts), model expression, and confirm their thoughts as valid and important.
NONVERBAL COMMUNICATION	Using nonverbal communication is efficient, represents a different medium, and creates an inclusive tone in your classroom. At the beginning of the year, your students can come up with three to five nonverbal signals to represent their thinking. Signals might represent: I agree, I have a question, I am thinking, I need a break, I am confused, or I need help. Students use these signals in unobtrusive ways and are able to communicate thinking, needs, and requests to you and to their peers. Varying the form of expression through signals allows all learners to express their thinking in tangible, accessible, and powerful ways. See Figure 1.6 as an example of a nonverbal chart to represent thinking.
VISUAL UNDERSTANDING THROUGH SKETCHING	Include art and visual representation as a medium for learning and expression. During instructional read-aloud, allow students to "sketch to stretch" to represent their thinking about the text through pictures. Or, demonstrate math solutions or process, scientific conclusions, and their understanding of a historical event through sketching or pictures. You might create historical murals so students can demonstrate their understanding of the nuances of a historical event (the causes of an event, and the effects shown through actions and the expressions on the faces of the patriots during the Boston Tea Party as an example). See Figures 1.7a and 1.7b as examples.
VISUAL UNDERSTANDING SCAFFOLDED THROUGH ORGANIZERS	Use visual organizers to express ideas and understanding. Quick and simple organizers provide all students, especially struggling students, with an accessible option for expressing ideas and understandings. Organizers can be premade or quickly made by students. One example is the "3-2-1"—three big ideas (from the book, experiment, lesson, concept), two questions, and one element or place where you need help. Another is a basic box with a line and bullets. On the line students jot the big idea (or conclusion or solution), and next to each bullet, they share details. See Figures 1.8 and 1.9 as examples of visual organizers.

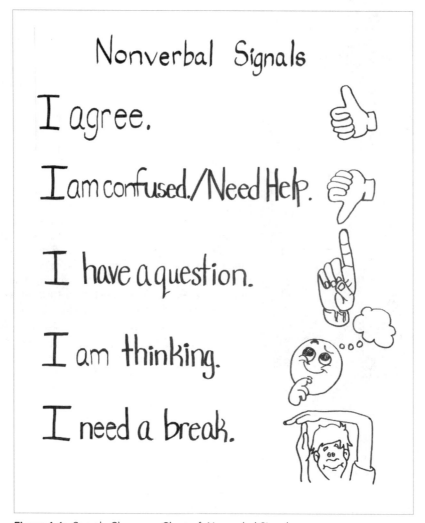

Figure 1.6: Sample Classroom Chart of Nonverbal Signals

Figure 1.7a–1.7b: Historical Mural of the Reasons Behind the Boston Tea Party

3-2-1 Thinking

3 Big Ideas

_____

_____

_____

_____

2 Questions

Q1 _____

_____

_____

Q2 _____

_____

_____

1 Way You Need Support

_____

_____

_____

_____

Figure 1.8: Visual Organizers That Can Demonstrate Understanding

BIG IDEA AND DETAILS ORGANIZER

Big Idea
Details:

Details:

-
-
-

Figure 1.9: Visual Organizers That Can Demonstrate Understanding

#5 *Embrace the Power of* Yet *(K–8)*

Believing in and teaching the transformative power of *yet* is perhaps my favorite of all moves. Life, learning, progress, and success is always about *yet*. What you can't do now is not what you can't do, but what you can't do *yet*.

Wrapping your mind around *yet* is not always easy. This summer, I got back into my yoga practice. Since I tend to go in and out of the practice, when I start back up, I am usually out of shape, and the yoga poses are hard for me. It doesn't help when I am sitting in child's pose (completely bent over, head and body on mat, lying there) and the guy next to me is in a one-handed plank (envision a one-handed push-up). I am unable to move, and the person next to me is basically supporting his body weight with one arm. But in yoga, the teacher says, "Yoga is about learning to fly. If you can't fly, run. If you can't run, walk. If you can't walk, crawl. Wherever you are is where you are. You will get there. Embrace where you are and believe that you will learn to fly." These words are exactly the kinds of words we need to say to our students.

Begin by acknowledging that students are where they are. Embrace that, and believe that they will learn how to fly. Truly. Believing in the power of *yet* is not some touchy-feely ideology but is grounded in the belief that when we have a mindset that trusts that all students can grow, we can move our students to a place of great joy and success.

For me, embracing *yet* is a four-part process:

1. **Acknowledge struggles.** Don't shy away from them; don't try to smooth them over or pretend they don't exist. Have honest and authentic conversations with students (developmentally appropriate to the age and maturity of the student), and let students know that it is absolutely okay that something is hard for them. Something is hard for everyone. Use yourself or other people students may know as an example or model. You could say: *I know that _____ doesn't come easily to you right now. That's okay. We all have something that doesn't come as naturally to us the first time we learn it. The trick is to keep at it, and use our community to support you. Remember how we were talking about how we all have strengths and struggles? And about how even famous people have struggles? Well, I want you to be thinking about that now. I think that _____ is feeling hard for you. Let's talk about that.*

2. **Rephrase their challenge as something that they cannot do yet.** Put language around the struggle, as a *yet* phrase, and discuss this with them. Perhaps even posit this as a goal or in connection with a positive. For example, *You cannot yet read that text you want to read independently, but you are able to identify the genre and text elements that you like, and so here are three texts that are just like that one you want to read. They will move you toward being able to read that text independently.*

3. **Set goals.** Setting goals is about moving students from *not yet* to *yes.* This can include really breaking down steps or providing them with a process that will enable them to reach their desired results. For example, if a student wants to read a text that is too complex for him to both understand and enjoy, then perhaps set a goal to eventually read that book and lay out books that will lead him to success. Lay out a trajectory of reading that gets him from the reader he is today to the reader he wants to be. Literally, set the goal to read the more complex text (*Harry Potter,* for example), and lay out the reading that will move him there (reading *Sea of Monsters,* then reading *The Forgotten Door,* and then moving to read *The Secret Garden*).

4. **Celebrate.** We have far too few celebrations in our classrooms, and celebration is key to moving struggling learners. Celebrate milestones, celebrate successes, and definitely celebrate hard work. We don't necessarily have to achieve something to celebrate. I am not talking about "carrots and sticks" or any type of external reward, but a celebration of their work. Hard work is just that—hard to accomplish, but it will lead to success. At the end of yoga class, there is *shavasana.* It is a few quiet moments at the end of class where you sit on your mat in quiet meditation and acknowledge all your hard work. You will

pull your knees to your chest in a hug, bow to yourself, and acknowledge your work on the mat for that day. Remember to create moments of *shavasana* in your classrooms to acknowledge and celebrate the hard work of our students to move them from where they are and what they can't do yet to where they want to be.

KEEP IN MIND

Considering the environment is the first set of moves that will support struggling learners. To ensure the environment supports our students in the most positive way, keep in mind a few key ideas across grade levels and across disciplines:

- Represent ideas in simple ways. This would include using images for directions and anchor charts, and color-coding areas of the room.

- Organize materials so that they are accessible and can be found independently.

- Set and post goals daily. Be sure students are always clear about what is expected and what they are going to do.

CHAPTER TWO

*H*arness the Power of Collaborative Learning

It is late winter, and my fourth-grade students are moving through our inquiry into the American Revolution. We are studying this event through the lens of a child—something they came up with after learning that study through a particular lens adds texture to an inquiry into a historical time period. My students are excited as we gear up for another round of group work in which they will create a historical mural depicting the effect of the Revolution on young adolescents.

My students are already talking about how the groupings will work, and per our usual protocol, they will self-select topics and group members. I overhear a group of three boys talking about how they hope Doug will be in their group. This makes me smile. Doug is an amazing student (I believe they all are!), but he is also a struggling learner. He was a nonreader at the beginning of the year, and although he is making great progress, he still reads far below the level of a typical fourth-grade student. But these boys really want to have Doug in their group. Why? Our classroom is a community of collaborators. My students have interacted with peers in many contexts, and through these experiences they've come to realize that each learner has something to offer and is a valuable member of a group. In fact, Doug is known as our best "big thinker" because his ability to determine big ideas or see outside the box is unparalleled. Doug in turn loves group work and excels when he is working with his peers.

When we provide opportunities for struggling students to participate in peer learning, they have positive and successful experiences. In one study of the benefits of cooperative endeavors with struggling students it was gleaned, "Equally prominent in the teachers' beliefs was that cooperative learning provides struggling students with a more secure, less stressful learning environment. One teacher expressed this as, 'They [special education students] like the feeling of success that comes out a

16

lot in cooperative learning. . . .There's less frustration and anxiety'" (Jenkins, Antil, Wayne, and Vadasy 2003).

After many years of incorporating collaborative learning in my classroom—sometimes successfully, sometimes not—I have come to realize a few moves that will not only make collaborative learning successful but will also harness the power of collaborative learning to support all types of learners.

#6 *Practice Collaborative Work in Centers (K–8)*

Create collaborative structures that can happen across the year, in multiple contexts. I like to call these "over and over" structures, which means that students have frequent opportunities to work with peers and to practice working collaboratively in low-stakes situations.

One structure for daily peer work is the learning center. We frequently associate these with primary classrooms, but they are equally effective in upper-elementary and middle school classrooms. Centers can be used across the curriculum and offer opportunities to work with peers to learn concepts. For example, when studying a new genre in writing, you might use centers to immerse students in the genre. Each center would have a different lens, but all would work to engage students in collaborative reading, writing, speaking, and listening around the genre. See Figure 2.1 for an example of centers in a memoir unit.

GENRE: NARRATIVE UNIT—MEMOIR	
Center 1: Read-Aloud Students listen to texts read aloud (digitally) or take turns reading aloud mentor texts while other students chart what they notice about the sound of the genre and the way memoirs can both freeze and slow down time or move across it.	**Center 2: Craft** Students reread mentor texts to identify craft elements or notice patterns across texts or authors. Students can discuss craft elements and make a list.
Center 3: Author Study Students study one author closely. They can explore biographical/autobiographical information, talk about plot/character similarities, or notice craft elements across books.	**Center 4: Idea Study** Students reread mentor texts to study memoir topics. Based on what they learn, students mine their own lives and jot down ideas for their own memoir.

Figure 2.1: Possible Centers in a Memoir Unit

You can use centers in content area learning as well. In Figure 2.2, the centers represent different elements of the discipline, complete with different tools and modalities of learning.

REVOLUTIONARY WAR INQUIRY CENTERS	WEATHER UNIT CENTERS
Center 1: Geography Maps, globes, and historical murals.	**Center 1: Instruments** Materials to make weather tools; tools to predict, measure, and analyze weather; materials for experiments.
Center 2: Biography Short texts, longer biographies, picture quality books, timelines, video clips, photographs, and other artifacts depicting information about important people from the time period.	**Center 2: Observation** Tangible objects and artifacts that can be used to observe and predict weather, books, technology (including sites, photos, apps, and video clips) depicting various weather patterns.
Center 3: Primary Sources Historical artifacts and photographs, as well as tools that can help students read, examine, and analyze the primary sources (such as magnifying glasses, definitions of words particular to the time period).	**Center 3: Wondering and Research** Class wondering board, KWL (see Chapter 4 for updated version) and various texts, both print and digital, with which to wonder, ask questions, hypothesize, conduct research, jot notes, and have conversations.
Center 4: Big Idea Texts, research, primary sources, graffiti wall, and other artifacts of conversations. In addition, bring essential questions from the unit into the conversation. Students examine the possible lenses through which to study the Revolution—the role of women, the role of adolescent, and so on—in order to come up with some big ideas about the unit of study.	**Center 4: Big Idea** Various texts about weather-related issues, from storms, to global warming, to issues with weather tracking and predicting. Students use these artifacts to generate thinking about scientific crosscutting concepts and real-world weather-related issues. Bring essential questions from the unit to the conversations.

Figure 2.2: Possible Content Area Centers

When students work in centers, use the following guidelines:

- Students are engaged in an authentic exercise/activity that is meaningful and relevant. I choose to use the words *exercise* and *activity* rather than *task*, as I am first and foremost providing students with an authentic opportunity to collaborate.

- The exercise/activity is not time bound. That way, students won't have to worry about not finishing or what to do if they finish early.

- Students have a protocol that guides how the center group works together.

- Always discuss the exercise/activity at hand. What is the activity? What are we doing? How will we get started? Do we have any questions? Has another group been to this center? What is their thinking?

- Decide how the activity will go. Each student needs to understand the activity and participate. For example, if students need to read a text, will they do this as a group, in pairs, or independently? If students are exploring an artifact, what tool will they need?

- Use phrases to engage all group members. Teach students to use phrases such as, "What do you think, _____?" or, "_____, do you agree?" or, "_____, what did you find?"

This protocol supports struggling learners because expectations are clear, steps are outlined, and authentic collaborative scaffolds are naturally built in. All these elements contribute to success. Try to avoid assigning teacher-created roles. For example, it is not productive to create a "vocabulary detective" (one person in charge of vocabulary) or "weather recorder" (one person in charge of recording weather data). Instead, center protocols should allow all students to learn and take part. See Figures 2.3 and 2.3b for pictures of collaborative centers.

Figure 2.3a, 2.3b: Literacy Collaborative Centers

When using centers to support collaboration, the teacher's role is to:

- Plan engaging, relevant centers that serve as a collaborative learning experience to support *all* learners in a particular unit of study. The easiest way to do this is to implement the same four centers across the year or in different units of study. For example, in writing I usually have the following centers: author highlight/study, ideas study, craft study, and read-aloud. In primary grades (K, 1), I have literacy centers: library center (for book shopping, shared reading, independent, and/or partner reading), writing centers (with lots of tools from the class writing center, including premade books and materials to make writing in various genres), language play center (materials to sort and make letters, words, and sentences; word study games that reinforce phonemic awareness, phonics, and sight word reading), and a listening center (digital reading, listening to texts read aloud). In social studies: geography, biography, primary sources, and big idea. In science: scientific instruments (making instruments, conducting experiments), observation, wondering and research, and big idea.

- Support students in centers. I usually have a flexible plan for how I will support learners. This means that I plan for specific teaching moves I will bring to the centers but am flexible enough to allow for time to support the issues/needs that I may not have anticipated.
- Implement small-group instruction. The support I give learners in centers is a type of small-group instruction. During this time, I use the following protocol:
  - ➤ **Observe:** Notice what students are doing in the center. Look for specific elements that correspond with recent teaching and learning. Use your observations and unit goals to make decisions about what to teach.
  - ➤ **Instruct:** Provide students a relevant teaching point that can be practiced in the center. Be sure your teaching point is short, five to ten minutes at most, so that students can continue to collaborate and learn together in the center.
  - ➤ **Support Practice:** As always, actively engage students as you ask them to try on the teaching point. You might want to model what you're asking them to do. Support and direct as necessary.
  - ➤ **Take Notes:** Be sure to record both observations and teaching points. See Chapters 5 and 10 for sample record keeping forms.

More information about supporting learners through small-group instruction can be found in Chapter 5.

#7 Establish a Culture of Collaboration to Support Peer Learning (1–8)

When you establish a culture of collaboration, you create a community where students not only know how to work together but also value working with each and every member of the community. This culture supports struggling learners in a variety of ways. First, learning becomes collaborative, and all learners benefit from the collective brainpower in the room. Next, learners have a go-to person when in need. Going to a co-learner is an excellent problem-solving strategy that a learner can use when in need. And third, and possibly most important, is that students are learning collaboration skills. As identified through a variety of research, including through a survey of fifteen hundred of the world's CEOs, the need to collaborate with peers is considered an essential skill for academic and career success (Palmisano 2010).

For learners to find value in working with a variety of students, create opportunities for students to get to know each other. During the first month of school, make sure students work with each and every other student in the class. I monitor this by creating a grid of their names and ask that they work with another student for a short period of time each day. Students may meet with another learner to go over their homework from the night before, talk about their independent reading text (this is how I got students into productive and well-matched reading partnerships!), or work together to read and discuss a page in a social studies or science text. Any activity will do because the primary goal is to collaborate with another student.

I refer to this as speed partnering; it's kind of like speed dating. The goal is to get to know each student in a collaborative context and work with every other student, even for just five or ten minutes. After each partnership experience, ask students to discuss or record one positive thing about their partner and/or the experience of working with that partner. This solidifies the idea that we all have something to contribute to collaborative tasks. Then record a check in the box that shows the intersection of the two names. The next day, students experience working with another student. We do this for about three weeks (for me it is the first month of school) until every student has "partnered up" with every other student at least once. See Figure 2.4 for an example of a class grid.

To foster a culture of collaboration, allow students to have a say in partnerships and groupings. In doing so, you'll let your students know that you value their input and that you trust they will make positive and inclusive decisions.

What might this collaboration look like? After introducing students to a new collaborative experience, ask them to jot a note to identify students they want to work with (provide parameters: how many students, what the experience will be, how long they will be working together). Then ask them to write the names of the students and why they want to work with them. For example, consider Doug from the chapter's opening anecdote. Eric could record Doug's name and, next to his name, record the reasons why he wants to work with Doug. He might write that Doug is great at determining the effect of an event (something that is integral to the task of creating a historical mural), notices details, and also draws really well. Eric would then list the names of other students and why he wants to work with them as well.

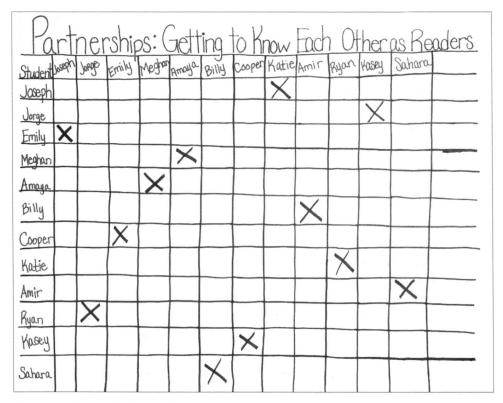

Figure 2.4: Partnership Class Grid

I take the students' requests and make final decisions about partnerships and groups. My decision honors their thinking, even if I need to adjust some of the participants in a group or partnership. Early on I establish that I am balancing their voices with my own understanding about their strengths and what they can learn from each other.

Always consider group dynamics and balancing chemistry with skills. When you come from the belief that each student has something to offer, and that struggling students should not be in collaborative contexts just as a mentee, then you create a classroom culture where all students can be successful in peer learning experiences.

Another way to build a culture of collaboration is to create a room of experts, so students can support each other. At the beginning of the year, we work hard to get to know each other as writers. As we learn about each writer's strengths, we add their names and expertise to an expert board. I make sure to identify an expertise for each writer, and I celebrate the ways in which they could support each other.

For example, even though Doug was an emergent reader, he had a gift for listening to a piece of writing and getting his peers to say more. He would point to parts that needed more dialogue or character description. Sometimes he might suggest that the writer add more information about the setting. He was the perfect partner during the brainstorming or revising stages. He knew how to ask the writer questions and offered suggestions for where and how to write more.

#8 *The Power of Two: Use Partnerships (K–8)*

One could argue that partnerships are the most powerful collaborative structure available to us. Having a peer in academic endeavors supports the development of executive functioning skills such as planning and preparing for learning. It supports task initiative and even supports comprehension and composition development. In fact, even a small amount of collaboration, such as talking for five or ten minutes with a peer about a text, is shown to have a dramatic impact on student understanding and meaning-making (Fall, Webb, and Chudowsky 2000).

Why is collaboration so powerful? There are many reasons one can point to, but for me, it traces back to Lev Vygotsky and his beliefs about social learning. "You can do alone tomorrow what you can do together today" is an adage attributed to Vygotsky's beliefs around a "more knowledgeable other." In a partnership, a learner is supported as she grapples with new ideas and is simultaneously introduced to the ideas, beliefs, and understandings of another. This other perspective positively affects the learner and enables her to integrate new and deeper levels of understanding.

As a classroom teacher, I used partnerships across the curriculum but found them essential to reading, writing, and math. It is important to understand that reading and writing partners work best when they are more homogeneous rather than heterogeneous. For struggling learners, this is particularly important. We don't use partnerships so that struggling learners can be mentored by another learner; we use partnerships so that we can harness the power of social learning to support all students. The belief that every reader or writer is capable of supporting another reader or writer is a key to success. Figure 2.5 shows how you might incorporate partnerships in reading across grades K–8. See Figure 2.6 for suggestions on how to use partnerships in writing.

WHAT DO STUDENTS READ?	HOW ARE THE TEXTS READ AND DISCUSSED?
Grades K–1 • Same book, one copy shared between partners **Grades 2–8** • Different book, by interest • Different book, same topic • Different book, same series • Different book, same author • Same book, two copies (same book partnerships) • Book my partner just read	**Grades K–1** • See-saw reading (taking turns by page or part) • Choral reading (read at the same time) • Echo reading • Dramatic reading (taking on different characters' voices) • During and after reading, partners talk about the books **Grades 2–8** • Reading is done alone, based on individual pacing and goals • Partners come together to talk about the books before and/or after reading

Figure 2.5: How to Incorporate Partnerships in Reading Across Grades

STAGES OF WRITING	HOW PARTNERS CAN HELP
Generating Ideas	Brainstorm together; remind your partner to use the big three: people, places, and things.
Rehearsal	Brainstorm together or help a partner flesh out and organize an idea.
Generating Writing/ Developing Writing	Suggest a strategy for getting started or for developing an idea; be a sounding board for sharing writing.
Drafting	Together make a plan for getting the idea down on the page.
Revising	Note what is working well in the writing, find parts to revise, make suggestions for what and how to revise.
Craft (part of revision)	Refer back to mentor texts, and suggest some craft moves to try in the draft.
Editing	Make suggestions about spelling, punctuation, or other conventions.
Publishing	Be an audience for your partner; celebrate together!

Figure 2.6: How to Use Partnerships in Writing

There are many ways to get students into partnerships. You can either allow students to choose their partner or choose for them. I have done both, successfully, and believe that both can work to support struggling learners.

If you decide to choose reading and writing partners for your students, I suggest the following steps:

1. Begin the year with the speed partnering protocol (discussed earlier).

2. Gather information on each learner's strengths, weaknesses, level of reading or writing, and interests.

3. Use the information you glean from this experience to determine partnerships. Let students know who their partner is and why you have chosen to put them together. *Emily and Sam, you both like reading mysteries. I think you will have some great partner conversations about the books you are reading. David, you are great at getting writing going, and Maddie, you are excellent at making suggestions for revisions. I think you can really help each other with your individual strengths across the writing process.*

4. Teach one or two lessons per unit of study on how to be a helpful partner.

5. Provide students with checklists that can help them to reflect on their partnership and support each other as learners.

See Figure 2.7 for an example of a partnership checklist.

If you allow students to choose their own reading and writing partners, I suggest the following steps:

1. Begin the year with the speed-partnering protocol.

2. Gather information on each learner's strengths, weaknesses, level of reading or writing, and interests.

3. Have students reflect on the partnership experiences, noting ways in which he or she works well with other learners.

4. Ask students to use the information gleaned from the partner experiences to make suggestions on who they would like to be their reading or writing partner. Ask students to record at least three names of students and why they wish to work with them. This information is given directly to you.

5. Make a final decision on partnerships. Share this information with students.

6. Teach one or two lessons per unit of study on how to be a helpful partner.

7. Provide students with checklists that can help them to reflect on their partnership and support each other as learners.

See Figure 2.7 for an example of a partnership checklist.

PARTNER CONVERSATION CHECKLIST	NOT YET	I'M TRYING	YES!
I prepared for my partner conversation by reading, jotting, and thinking about the book.			
I demonstrated active listening by facing my partner and showing interest.			
I participated in the conversation by sharing ideas, asking questions, and making connections to my partner's ideas.			

Figure 2.7: Partner Conversation Checklist

#9 *Model Collaboration by Using a Fishbowl Technique (K–8)*

We create successful collaborations for our struggling students when we model the behaviors and skills that they need to know to be successful during group work. One effective way to model is to fishbowl a group working together. After observing a group, deconstruct how and why the group worked or didn't work well together and brainstorm ways they can improve.

For example, a second-grade classroom was launching reading clubs. I decided to conduct a fishbowl lesson in order to model (in an engaging and active way) what a successful reading club would look and sound like. I asked the club reading about ocean animals to conduct their group meeting in the center of the class meeting area. The rest of the class formed a larger circle around the ocean animals club. I asked the club to conduct their meeting while the other students observed and noted what was happening. I called them my inner circle (ocean animals club) and outer circle (the rest of the students in the class). As the ocean animals club talked, I watched and called time-outs to do the following:

- Ask questions. By asking questions of the inner circle, I was pushing their thinking or asking them to explain why they were doing what they were doing.
- Model something quickly. I modeled how to extend the conversation or dip back into the text to extend meaning.

- Check in with the outer circle. I had to make sure that my outer circle was following and digesting the model, so I paused a few times to check in with them. I either asked rhetorical questions, such as "Did you notice what Ellory just did?" or quietly noticed aloud what the inner circle was doing while I was looking directly at the outer circle. I would say things like, "That was great, Jose. Asking Emma to clarify is a good way to check your understanding and helps her as well."

- Restate essential ideas. When a student shared an idea that was essential to the book, I reinforced it by restating.

See Figure 2.8 as an example of a fishbowl.

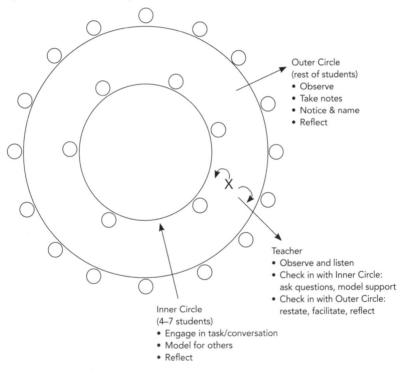

Outer Circle
(rest of students)
- Observe
- Take notes
- Notice & name
- Reflect

Teacher
- Observe and listen
- Check in with Inner Circle:
  ask questions, model support
- Check in with Outer Circle:
  restate, facilitate, reflect

Inner Circle
(4–7 students)
- Engage in task/conversation
- Model for others
- Reflect

Figure 2.8: An Example of a Fishbowl

Sometimes I scaffolded the club's talk by whispering into one student's ear, providing that child with specific direction or feedback. I might offer the exact words or questions to ask. This quick model, quietly directed at an individual student, is quite successful with struggling students as they take on and own my direction/feedback. After a few minutes, I turned to my outer circle and asked them to name what they saw. We recorded some notes on a T-chart—one side recording what the group did well, the other side recording issues, problems, or what the group could work on. We then brainstormed next steps.

In this particular second-grade class, fishbowling one group showed other clubs how their conversation should look and sound. Here are the basic steps for fishbowling in any grade or content area:

1. Decide what you want to model, and choose a group of students who will be the "fish" or inner circle for the exercise.

2. Review the protocol for fishbowls with students. In general, the inner circle conducts their group as they normally would, and the outer circle observes the inner circle and notes what they see and hear. Students in the outer circle may choose to observe one specific student or the entire group. Students can jot notes or observe and be ready to discuss findings.

3. Ask the inner circle to begin their work together. The group might already have a plan for how to start, or they might need a guiding question. Facilitate as necessary. When considering support for struggling learners, be sure to incorporate time-outs when you can ask questions, model something, check in with the outer circle, or restate essential ideas.

4. Reflect with all learners. Create a T-chart that documents what the inner circle did well (that all learners want to emulate) and some suggestions for what the groups can also do. This information can be used to create reading or book clubs plans or can even be used to create rubrics or checklists of the success criteria for productive and collaborative conversations. Students should have the opportunity to be in both the inner circle and the outer circle.

#10 *Scaffold Student Talk with Scripted Options (2–8)*

Group learning is essential and productive but certainly not easy. One way to scaffold student talk during group work is to provide some scripted talk options in the form of sentence stems. Begin by modeling how to use the sentence stems in conversations. You can:

- Find a partner to model talk. You might ask another teacher to help you or find a student who can model this with you in front of the class.

- Demonstrate using the suggested sentence stems in a conversation. The conversation can be about a book, content topic, a piece of writing, and so on.

- Provide students with anchor charts, both class (enlarged) and/or individual (4 × 6 or 8 × 11), of possible sentence stems that they can use to start and move conversations along.

See Figure 2.9 for some possible sentence stems.

Sentence Stems for Clarifying:

Our task is _____.

Can you say more about _____?

I have a question about _____.

What should we do first?

Can someone explain _____?

Sentence Stems for Sharing an Opinion:

I think that we should _____.

My opinion is _____.

I believe that _____.

Based on _____, I think _____.

In the text it said _____, and I think _____.

Sentence Stems for Providing Feedback or Making Suggestions:

I like _____; you could _____.

What about if you _____?

Why don't you try _____?

Sentence Stems for Agreeing with Another/Piggybacking on an Idea:

I agree that _____.

I also think that _____.

I agree with _____ because _____.

Sentence Stems for Disagreeing:

I hear what you are saying, but I think _____.

_____ thinks _____. My opinion is that _____.

Another way to look at it is _____.

I used to think _____; I now think _____.

Figure 2.9: Possible Sentence Stems

After introducing and modeling the sentence stems, give students time to practice with the tool provided. Make sure each student has a practice partner, and offer a possible topic of conversation. It's best to choose a topic they can all speak to and one that will spark conversation. They might talk about a recent read-aloud, their own independent reading texts, their own writing, a school event, or something in the news. With practice, students will build up their understanding around how and when to use certain sentence stems. They might even come up with their own phrases. Doug started with the phrase, "I hear what you are saying, but I think. . . ." and moved to the phrase, "I hear what you are saying, but think about this. . . ." He took the stem, understood its intent was to acknowledge another person's thinking, and put forth his own. He put his own Doug spin on it!

#11   *Introduce Student Work Plans (2–8)*

Collaboration tools work well with struggling learners because they provide tangible materials that support them as they manage partnership and group work. One of my favorite tools is a student work plan. A student work plan is part agreement, part planner, and its role is to lay out the work in a mutually agreeable way. The planner contains information about the work, notes the plan for working together, and asks each group member to sign off. See Figure 2.10 for an example of a book club planner.

You can use a student work plan in a variety of disciplines and contexts, but this tool is especially effective for book clubs. One group of fourth-grade readers had a problem sticking to the agreed-upon plan. Although the group had chosen to work together and created the plan for reading, most had trouble sticking to the plan and working in a collaborative way. Two in particular, Harrison and Jason, could frequently be found arguing about the reading, the response, the conversation . . . basically everything. This is when I decided that each student needed to have his own work plan, and that they would put their name at the bottom of the planner. When students sign their names, they feel more accountable and take the plan more seriously. The visual and concrete nature of the plan increases student agency and supports struggling learners.

Student work planners can also be in the form of a checklist. Checklists work better for some struggling learners because they are organized visual tools that require the student to "check-in" on how they are doing and where they need to go next. In fact, checklists can serve as a mechanism for feedback and enable students to answer the three questions that researcher John Hattie suggests effective

BOOK CLUB PLANNER

CLUB NAME _____   DATES _____

BOOK TITLE _____

AUTHOR _____   GENRE _____

OUR PLAN:
READING PLAN

MONDAY	TUESDAY	WEDNESDAY	THURSDAY	FRIDAY

CONVERSATION PLAN

_____

_____

_____

_____

SIGNATURES

_____   _____

_____   _____

Figure 2.10: Student Book Club Planner

feedback answers: *Where am I going? How am I going?* and *Where am I going next?* (Hattie 2009). Checklists can be used to support the process or the content and work best if they include deadlines. Figures 2.11 and 2.12 are examples of student planners in the form of checklists.

TASK (OR ELEMENT)	SIGN OFF
I understand the group project and what we are creating.	
I know the due date of the project. It is _____.	
I know my role. I will _____ by _____.	
I know my role. I will _____ by _____.	
I have scheduled a conference with my teacher. It is _____.	
(After conferring with your teacher) Next, I need to _____ _____.	

Figure 2.11: Process Checklist

TASK (OR ELEMENT)	SIGN OFF
I know the group task. In my own words, it is _____ .	
My role is _____ .	
My first job is to _____ .	
My next job is to _____ .	
My last job is to _____ .	

Figure 2.12: Content Checklist

The checklists in Figures 2.11 and 2.12 are intended to be used by individual students. Individual checklists don't replace group forms, but they serve a different purpose. Struggling students often have weak executive functioning skills—skills that drive planning, managing, and controlling tasks and emotions—and collaborative work can be especially challenging. With group planners, struggling students will typically "go along to get along," and the checklist is usually managed by other students. Individual checklists give students a place to go to check their understanding, set goals, identify success criteria, plan for their tasks and role within the group, get feedback from themselves and others, and manage their time in relation to the task—all essential steps to positive and successful collaborations.

KEEP IN MIND

Collaborations can be positive experiences for all students, including struggling learners. Keep in mind what I call my top three ways to ensure collaborations go well.

#3: Plan to coach collaborations. I find that group work works best when the teacher envisions herself as a coach: one who does not get in the game to play but feels that she has a role in calling time-outs or calling practice. We don't want a laissez-faire mentality for group learning; we want to maintain the mindset of a facilitator who keeps goals and objectives front and center yet allows student agency and choice to drive the work.

#2: Be willing to go to plan B. One of my favorite pieces of advice was what my staff developer called "planning not to plan" when teaching. This means that even with all these moves, there will be the need for the occasional adjustments. Embrace that. Students are all unique and different, and the only thing consistent with struggling learners is that they have many inconsistencies. Strategies or tools that have worked before may need an adjustment or tweaking to continue to work successfully.

#1: Let the work unfold. I am not sure when being a constructivist educator became a four-letter word, but allowing work to unfold organically is what is most natural to all learners. That means that group dynamics will play a part in the learning as well as the way the learning unfolds. Allow these elements to occur. I especially keep an eye out for students to take on leadership roles in the classroom. For example, Doug might take the lead in getting his group started for the day and wrap up with a recap of what they accomplished. Harrison might be the unofficial "conversation starter" for his book club. What's powerful is that these roles unfolded organically in the classroom and were embraced by all of the learners.

CHAPTER THREE

Use Visuals in Teaching and Learning

In 325 BC, the great philosopher Aristotle claimed, "Thought is impossible without an image." The same can be said for teaching and learning in 2017. Paivio's dual coding theory (1986) supports the notion that learning happens when there is a confluence between visual and verbal stimuli. This notion continues to be supported today. In John Hattie's meta-analysis of learning styles found in *Visible Learning*, he concluded that all learners benefit from multiple means of learning and that struggling students benefit from reducing the low cognitive load (Hattie 2009). Providing visuals becomes even more imperative, as coupling auditory information with visual elements will enable students with learning differences to process information more effectively.

Visuals have never been as accessible to us as educators as they are today, thanks to the technology tools in today's classrooms. Visuals can be used in a variety of ways: to illustrate new and complex content, introduce new and/or academic vocabulary, demonstrate scientific concepts, illustrate the setting of a text or a scene of historical significance, represent a number or algorithm in math, capture instruction and learning, or provide a scaffold for written composition and response. When we incorporate visuals into lessons, we support learners as they grapple with new ideas. They also motivate and engage learners. In addition, visuals serve as a touchstone for learning and can be referenced by learners after a lesson. They support "stickability" in learning—the ability to comprehend and retain information and learning—a prevalent issue for most struggling learners.

The pedagogical approach of chunk and chew has taught us that for every eight to ten minutes of instruction (chunk), students should interact with the information (chew) for one to two minutes. Why is this the case? Our working memories (the part of the brain where we temporarily hold information until it can be processed and stored in long-term memory) can hold only seven (plus or minus two) pieces of information (Miller 1956). For our struggling students, many of whom have less developed working memories and auditory processing challenges, that first eight to ten minutes is less meaningful without the accompaniment of visual aids. Therefore, our classrooms should be places where visuals are used in both teaching and learning.

#12 *Incorporate Virtual Field Trips (K–8)*

One visual learning tool is the virtual field trip. A virtual field trip is a site that allows learners to "visit" a time, place, or habitat that they would not typically be able to experience in person. Virtual field trips engage students in five- to seven-minute trips of both visual and auditory stimuli. Many use video, photographs, and images, but others use charts, maps, graphs, and other visual tools as well. Some virtual field trips can be accessed at no cost, while some have a subscription fee. Figure 3.1 shows some of my favorites.

RESOURCE	SITE DESCRIPTION AND POSSIBLE USE
Scholastic: www.scholastic.com/teachers /student-activities	This free portion of the Scholastic website offers a variety of tools for teaching. Titled "activities," these tools range from photographs, to animated videos, interview transcripts, and virtual field trips. Each activity offers possibilities for classroom use as: • The warm-up to a lesson: The visual can be used to engage and connect students to content and build an interest in the topic or lesson. • The lesson itself: Integrate the visual into the lesson itself to demonstrate a teaching point or share information. The visual is peppered with teacher talk, student turn and talks, or information. • A learning center: Using the visual in a learning center will enable students to build knowledge as they interact with the visual in a collaborative setting.

Figure 3.1: Virtual Field Trip Resources

(continues)

Figure 3.1 *(continued)*

RESOURCE	SITE DESCRIPTION AND POSSIBLE USE
OnlineUniversites.com: www.onlineuniversities.com/blog/ 2010/01/100-incredible-educational-virtual-tours-you -dont-want-to-miss/	OnlineUniversities.com has a fantastic curated list of virtual tours that can be used for teaching and learning. Their list includes cities, famous buildings and landmarks, museums, college campuses, outer space, how things are made, humans and animals, baseball stadiums, theme parks, and Google Earth Virtual Tours. This site can be used to build background knowledge before a lesson or unit of study. For example, envision taking students on a virtual tour to explore the setting of a book, the scene of a historical event, or the location of a country or culture you are studying in social studies or foreign language class.
iTunes U: https://itunes.apple.com/us/app/ itunes-u/id490217893?mt=8	This application can be found in the iTunes store and is a resource that allows you to create lessons, hold online discussions, design tasks and assignments, and assess students. My favorite feature is the catalog of free educational content available for use from organizations and universities around the world. The app is free but requires an iPhone or iPad for use.
Virtual Field Trips.org: www.virtual fieldtrips.org	This is a subscription site of curriculum-based virtual field trips ready for classroom use. There are ready-made virtual field trips for social studies, geography, and life science topics. The field trips span a variety of topics and are made for grades K–12. Some teacher tools, including assessments, accompany the field trips. You might use this site to build background knowledge and vocabulary. While taking the virtual field trip, introduce new and pertinent vocabulary to students. Have students interact with the vocabulary while viewing the actual place, setting, or scientific concept. Ask students to turn and talk about the vocabulary, create a concept wheel or word splash representing the vocabulary. Capture the words on a vocabulary word wall for future use and reference.

#13 *Rethink Anchor Charts (K–8)*

A visual tool that is essential to teaching and learning is the anchor chart. Teachers have been using anchor charts for years, but these tools do not always support struggling learners. In fact, many times I see anchor charts that actually detract from the lesson because they visually overstimulate struggling learners. The key to using an anchor chart as a visual support for struggling learners is to adhere to the guidelines discussed next.

CONSIDER THE NUMBER OF ITEMS ON A CHART

It has been said that a list of more than four is a list too long, and the same is true of the amount of information on anchor charts. Anchor charts can potentially be created with too much information on them—a long list of strategies, a number of steps to a procedure, multiple ideas about a variety of subtopics. And while that might

During Writing Workshop, We Can:
- Start a new piece of writing.
- Go back and work on a piece of writing.
- Use our mentor texts to find ideas, inspirations and craft moves.
- Have a writing conference.

Figure 3.2: "Just Right" Anchor Chart

not negatively affect all learners, it can affect struggling learners. Why? Struggling learners can be easily overstimulated with visual, verbal, and tactile information. When we cram too much information onto anchor charts, we are no longer supporting learners with a visual tool; we may in fact be detracting from what the tool was meant to do: provide a visual tool during instruction, and create a visual artifact to use during independent practice. The key is to think three bears—not too little (enough to support the learners with tangible information), not too much (limit the amount of items/ideas on the anchor chart), but just right (information that represents your teaching, in pictures and words, that can be easily accessed during and after the lesson). See Figure 3.2 for an example of a "just right" anchor chart.

REMEMBER THE PURPOSE AND FUNCTION OF ANCHOR CHARTS

Anchor charts are not cute wall decorations or wallpaper. First and foremost, anchor charts are visual tools for teaching. This means that the anchor chart should be created *in* lessons *with* students. If we believe in the purpose of anchor charts, the first rule of thumb is to create or re-create anchor charts each year. It is great to save them (perhaps as photos) as a reminder of the visual tools you used in a unit of study, but know that last year's anchor chart is not relevant or helpful to this year's class. I usually look at the unit anchor chart pictures during a unit as a reminder of the charts I want to create, but then I create them in lessons with and for my current students. See Figure 3.3, What Writers Do, as an example of an anchor chart that can be recreated each year in a kindergarten classroom.

Figure 3.3: "What Writers Do" Anchor Chart from a Kindergarten Class

In addition, I want to make sure that purpose matches form and function. When I create "over time" anchor charts, I attend to the idea that they are running records of ideas for students. "Over time" anchor charts refer to those charts that develop over time, in more than one minilesson. For example, in reading at the beginning of the year, I might have an anchor chart that lists a few ways that students can choose books. That anchor chart titled "Ways We Choose Books" has a list of four ways to choose books. However, later in the year, I may want to highlight other strategies students can use to choose books, so I create another anchor chart with additional strategies, titled "More Ways We Choose Books."

While I stick to my "no more than four" rule for most anchor charts, if this is an anchor chart that captures a longer list of ideas and is created over time, I am willing to bend my rule. Figures 3.4a and 3.4b show an "over time" anchor chart with a format that considers all learners.

Another way I might do this is to synthesize information from multiple anchor charts and create a new anchor chart with just the pertinent information on it. For example, in a third-grade writing unit, teachers were unpacking the information genre in a unit of study. Throughout the study, various anchor charts captured the learning. For the second half of the unit of study, the teachers synthesized the big

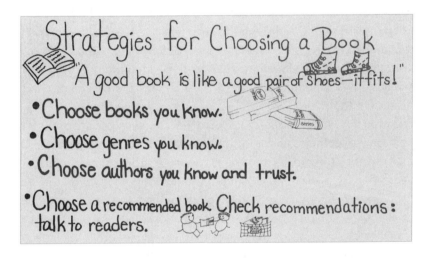

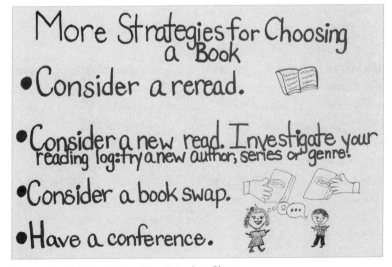

Figures 3.4a–3.4b: "Over Time" Anchor Charts

ideas from the unit and made this anchor chart the key anchor chart for the rest of the study. The key is to remember the purpose of the particular anchor chart, remember your learners, remember the rules of thumb surrounding the kinds of anchor charts that support struggling learners, and create a chart whose form will support all learners. Other tips for creating user-friendly and supportive anchor charts include using an alternating color to show the information over time (the color-coding system visually breaks up the words and supports all learners) and use short phrases or simple visuals so that the chart is not visually overstimulating.

PROVIDE STUDENTS WITH THEIR OWN COPIES OF ANCHOR CHARTS

As a classroom teacher, I considered many ways that visual tools could live in our classroom environment. Although I loved anchor charts (my nickname was "The Chart Queen"), I knew and understood how important it was not to overwhelm my struggling students with charts that contained too much writing and information. Occasionally I created 8.5-inch × 11-inch versions of anchor charts as individual student tools.

I first tried this with our classroom word wall. In my experience, students, especially struggling learners, seldom use word walls. They are way too far away, have too many words on them, and are hard to see. I made a simple, small, individualized word wall for my students. I limited the number of words on the student version, and I never included words they could not read and use. In addition, I added personally relevant words to each students' individual word wall—the names of their family members, places they visit often, words that other students remember but they themselves do not (or conversely, words they are ready to learn that their peers are not). The individual word wall can live in a variety of places: the back of their writing folders, inside their writing folders, laminated on top of their desks, or on the back cover of their writer's notebook.

I also created individual student copies of visual tools that captured strategies that were important for students to remember and access over time. Examples include: a short list of how we can spend our time during writing workshop, a list of writing strategies to generate and develop writing (free-write, lift a line, write in the margin, and so on [For more information on these strategies, see Chapter 8]), math strategies (guess and check, draw a table, draw a picture), an editing checklist, or specific examples of an author's craft. In each notebook, students had a section called "Tools" in which they attached their individual visual tools. For younger students, these tools can go into a section of their writing folder, can be glued to the front or back of the folders, or can go into the table caddies that house the materials students need during writing workshop. That way, students always have these visual tools at their fingertips. These are offshoots of the anchor chart but much more accessible! Figures 3.5a and 3.5b are examples of individual anchor charts. 3.5a is a checklist rendition of the anchor chart in Figure 3.2. 3.5b is a replica of the anchor chart in Figure 3.2, but in checklist format. It has boxes to check off the plan, and a place for student reflection. Figure 3.5c shows how a teacher could create an individual anchor chart for students.

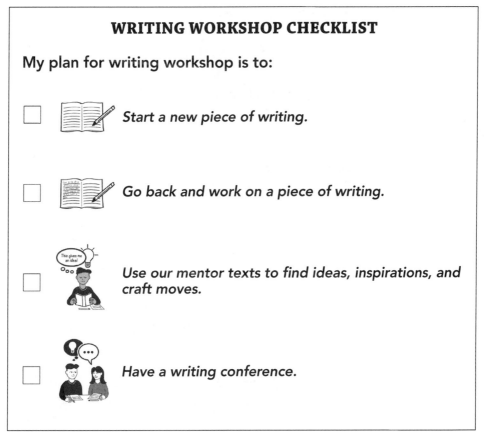

Figure 3.5a: Individual Anchor Chart

MAKE SURE ANCHOR CHARTS ARE ACCESSIBLE

Always, our audience is our students, but in particular, our audience is our struggling learners. This means that we are considering not just how we create the anchor charts but where we keep them. Are our visual tools accessible to all students?

When creating paper anchor charts, put the anchor chart paper on an easel. This allows you to transcribe the ideas and allows students to have a focal point at eye level. When the anchor chart is complete, consider where it will be accessed and stored. *Some* anchor charts can be placed on bulletin boards and walls for future

WRITING WORKSHOP CHECKLIST

My plan for writing workshop is to:

☐   *Start a new piece of writing.*

☐   *Go back and work on a piece of writing.*

☐   *Use our mentor texts to find ideas, inspirations, and craft moves.*

☐   *Have a writing conference.*

How did my plan go? Rate how writing went for you today on a scale of 1–5.

1	2	3	4	5
Not well	Okay	Good	Great	Best Writing Workshop

Why?

_____

_____

What is my plan for our next writing workshop?

_____

_____

Figure 3.5b: Individual Anchor Chart with Reflection

reference by students. However, a year's worth of anchor charts should not live in the environment. Students can't possibly access all that information. Hang anchor charts as close as possible to the eye level of your learners. This is important for all students, but particularly for students in grades K–2. For our youngest learners, wall space that is higher than five feet is way above their sight line. Anchor charts should be in close proximity to the learners who will use them.

ROTATE ANCHOR CHARTS

Consider displaying one or two anchor charts for a set period of time. As a classroom teacher, I used two metal rings to create a stack of anchor charts. The metal rings open and closed easily so I could add and remove anchor charts as needed. I hung this stack of charts on the side of the easel that was not facing the students. I had tangible evidence of my visual tools, and they could be easily accessed, yet I made the purposeful decision not to visually overstimulate my students by putting all those charts in the environment at once. Some anchor charts had a more permanent place in the room, but the rest were created, kept on the metal rings, and displayed when needed. Identify a prominent location in your classroom, and consider displaying two anchor charts per week or unit of study. These anchor charts are prominently displayed, in the same central and accessible location, and can be easily accessed by students. Figure 3.6 is an example of how first-grade teacher Crystal Tuozzolo features one anchor chart that is accessible to all students. In addition to the few prominently displayed anchor charts, Crystal stores all other anchor charts digitally and brings them up on her Smart Board if she needs to refer to them at a later date.

Figure 3.5c: Individual Anchor Chart and Class Anchor Chart

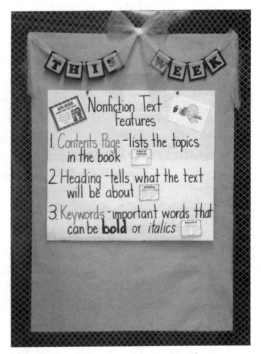

Figure 3.6: Easily Accessible Anchor Chart

#14 *Improve Retention with Sticky Note Prompts (1–8)*

Teachers can carry sticky notes (some premade and some made during a conference) to create annotations or supports for students. This visual tool can be used at any grade level in any discipline and can start as a tool that is introduced in a lesson and follows the student into independent practice.

For example, a first-grade collaborative classroom was studying persuasive writing. Before the lesson, the teacher and I brainstormed different ways to state an opinion. For the lesson to stick, we knew that proximity of learning materials matters. The Smart Board and the anchor chart were not close enough to students who needed additional support, so the special education teacher and I decided to use sticky note prompts. We created sticky note sentence strips that contained sentence stems, such as "I believe . . ." or "My opinion is . . ." or even, "I think or I like . . . ." These prompts are directly accessible, completely tangible, and can disappear or reappear as the learner needs them.

I also use sticky note prompts during conferences. One of the most frustrating moments for me early in my teaching career was when my students would forget the work that we did together in conferences. It was as if students were Teflon, and the teaching would slide right off.

Stickability, or retention of information, is a huge issue with struggling learners. Students come with a variety of learning issues (processing, attention, receptive communication), and many have a hard time holding on to information. A conference is a time when we can differentiate teaching and learning and interact with a learner at his or her own pace. However, a student might still have trouble holding on to the teaching point and applying it in reading and writing. In these situations, a visual can make all the difference.

I started jotting small notes on a sticky note to capture what we discussed and practiced during a conference. Occasionally I would do a quick sketch if I thought it would help. I leave the note with students as a reminder of what we discussed and to provide a quick example. For example, when conferring with second grader Emma, I focused on character work in her reading. I taught her the strategy C, T, E—take your character, name a trait, and find evidence—and jotted this on a sticky note. I gave her a few sticky notes with a T and an E for her to use while reading. She could either jot the trait and a piece of evidence or simply place the sticky note on the page as a reminder that she found the trait and some evidence on the page. I allowed her to decide since the note was to serve as a visual cue, not something that slowed down her reading.

I also used a sticky note prompt during a writing conference with Sam. Sam's writing was sketchy at best, with little detail given to the reader. I taught him the strategy of Say/Add One More Thing, using the specifics we discussed in whole class minilessons—writers add internal thinking, dialogue, or feelings to their writing. I made a few sticky note prompt reminders and placed them in two spots in his writing. He then went back to his writing to add to those places but could also move the note to other places in the writing and add there. Figures 3.7a, 3.7b, and 3.7c are examples of sticky note prompts from conferences.

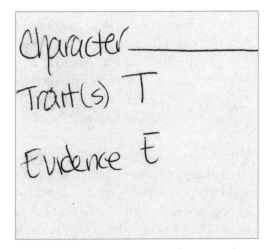

Figure 3.7a: Sticky Note Prompt from a Writing Conference Teaching the Strategy Say/Add One More Thing

Figure 3.7b: Sticky Note Prompt from a Reading Conference Teaching Second Grader Emma a Strategy for Thinking About her Characters

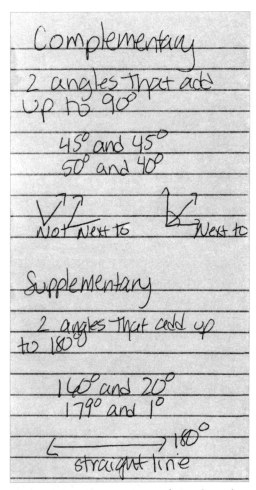

Figure 3.7c: Sticky Note Prompt from a Seventh-Grade Math Conference Teaching the Difference Between Supplementary and Complementary Angles

#15   *Offer Support with Formula, Cue, and Goal Cards (2–8)*

Formula cards are defined as visual prompt cards that contain vital information for solving equations or implementing steps in a process. Cue cards are mini-visuals that remind or cue students to remember concepts or ideas that were previously taught. Goal cards are small cards (such as index cards) that students use to self-identify how they will spend their time during independent practice. Formula, cue, and goal cards are examples of visual tools that provide struggling learners with tangible support during independent practice.

Formula cards can be used in any discipline but are especially useful during math and science. With formula cards, typically an approved accommodation for special needs students (but can work well as a scaffold for any struggling student), the "formula" is a necessary piece of information that a learner needs in order to complete a task. By providing a struggling learner with a formula card, you remove the obstacle of remembering the formula (or information) so that the learner can focus solely on application and usage. This scaffold works especially well in math and science because the formulas or definitions are a required first step to application and usage.

For example, Victoria, a fourth grade student who struggles with math, has formula cards to remember the difference between the associative, commutative, and identity properties. She accesses these cards from her "tool box" (which can simply be a pencil case, folder, or any other container used to house materials and supplies needed for the discipline) when answering questions or solving word problems involving these concepts. For Zach, an eighth grade student, his formula cards contain the definition of evaporation, transpiration, condensation, and crystallization as a sequence of processes in the water cycle. When he reads the weekly weather or interprets other weather data, he has the cards by his side to help him interpret the data accurately and use the content vocabulary in context. See Figure 3.8 for an example of a formula card.

Cue cards are great visual tools that students can use to remember strategies or processes in any discipline, but they work especially well in reading and writing. For example, teachers may want to provide students with cue cards that represent previous learning about reading and writing in various genres, steps in the writing process, or questions to ask/ways to talk during book club conversations. See Figure 3.9 as an example of cue cards that were used for second-grade book club conversations.

Associative Property

Numbers can "associate" or be grouped in different ways and the answer is the same.

Example
2+(3+4)=9
(2+3)+4=9

Identity Property

Numbers can show their "identity" and remain the same when a 0 is added to it.

Examples
5+0=5
3+0=3

Commutative Property

Numbers can "commute" or move around and the answer is the same.

Example
2+3=5
3+2=5

Figure 3.8: Formula Cards

Talk Prompts
(use for partnerships, reading clubs or book clubs)

Start with a retelling:

I am reading...
and I think...
In the book...
and I think...

Make Connections:

This reminds me of...
This (part, character, book) is just like...

Talk about Characters:

____ is a character who...
I noticed the characters...

Make Predictions:

My prediction is...
I think ____ will happen at the end of the book.

Ask Questions:

Why did...?
Do you think that...?

Figure 3.9: Cue Cards for Book Club Conversation

Goal cards are visual reminders of goals that students are working hard to accomplish. Goals can be short term (for the day or week) or longer term (for the unit or quarter). Writing down goals on cards gives students a visual reminder of how they will spend their time. Goal cards work particularly well when an image accompanies the written goal.

Goal cards can be used in any discipline, but they are especially useful during reading and writing workshop. For example, when students move from a reading or writing lesson, they may take or create a goal card for how they will use their time. The goal card simply and succinctly states what the goal is for the independent practice time. It is a short-term goal related to a recent lesson within unit. Some examples of goals follow:

- My goal is to work on my stamina and read for the entire independent reading time (20 minutes).

- My goal is to incorporate sensory images in my writing by describing what I was seeing and hearing.

- My goal is to note parts in my book when my character does something that reinforces a trait.

In addition to the stated goal, a goal card should contain a course of action for how a student will reach that goal. This is what I call the "so I need to" and is the strategy or plan of action for achieving the goal.

Students can also set goals that can be accomplished over a longer period of time, such as a unit or quarter. For example, one of my fourth grade students, Megan, set two goals for a unit of study. The first was around stamina; her goal was to maintain her focus and read for the entire independent reading time. Her "so I need to" was: be thoughtful about book choice (make sure it is interesting and will keep me reading), plan for short stopping points where I can retell in my mind or jot quickly on a sticky note, and push myself! Without the "so I need to," her goals were just lofty aspirations!

Pair goal setting with reflection (think book ends—one at the beginning and one at the end of your unit or quarter) so that the goal is clear, the process visible, the accomplishments acknowledged, and future goals set in accordance with what the learner still needs to work on. See Figure 3.10 for an example of Megan's goals.

Figure 3.10: Megan's Goals

#16 *Create Response Sheets (2–8)*

Response sheets are visual organizers for any kind of written response. They allow students to use visual elements to scaffold their process and record their thinking.

One type of visual organizer is an open-ended response sheet. An open-ended response sheet provides enough of a scaffold so that the student knows exactly what is being asked but open ended enough so that an appropriate challenge still exists.

For example, if students are asked to name three things that led to the Revolutionary War, you might accommodate the student response by creating visually organized response sheets like the one in Figure 3.11.

THREE REASONS THAT LED TO THE REVOLUTIONARY WAR ARE:

Reason 1: _____

Reason 2: _____

Reason 3: _____

For students who need a more supportive visual tool, provide a closed response format. Here's an example of a closed response about the Revolutionary War:

There were many reasons that led to the *Revolutionary War.* One reason was that

the colonists were taxed without having a say in government. This was called

_____. Another reason was _____

_____. A third reason was that *King George ordered British marines*

to _____.

Figure 3.11: An Example of a Response Sheet on the Revolutionary War

The key to using closed response sheets is to create outlines that are like cloze passages. Most of the information is on the page, but students need to add ideas or their own thinking. This modifies or scaffolds the listening and learning during a lesson. At the same time it sets up a learner to **own the learning** and **engage with the information**. It ensures that this tool does not become a crutch for students; instead, it supports them appropriately.

In both examples, the tools use various organizational elements to visually support output and written response of students. Although the examples were used in content areas (social studies and science), response sheets can be used in any discipline.

KEEP IN MIND

By considering the tools that can be used during direct instruction and independent practice, we create visual tools students can use throughout the learning process. We consider the learner by paying attention to the visual elements in materials/texts. Some general rules of thumb apply to visuals in learning tools:

- Use lines whenever possible. Many struggling learners have a hard time navigating open space on a page. They might feel constricted by a blank box or overwhelmed by a blank space beneath a question. Consider incorporating lines for: answers to constructed response questions, labels next to diagrams, and on maps (to show going from one location to another). You might even decide to use lined sticky notes.

- When using lengthy or complex discipline-specific texts, highlight a few key parts or sections. Consider highlighting text that contains little or no visual support, key words, or tables.

- Use graph paper instead of open space. This is an accommodation that helps students mostly in math, as the graph paper boxes help them to put numbers in appropriate boxes and line up information correctly. It can also be used in social studies or science when working with information in tables or charts.

- Number parts or paragraphs in lengthy text. This accommodation can help students break down reading, be used to refer to text parts clearly, or can be a point of reference for where information can be found.

CHAPTER FOUR

Scaffold Instruction Through Pre-Teaching

Many times in my life I have been quite startled at the beginning of a new experience—a car trip that took much longer and traveled through a much more rural area than expected, the beginning of a book that surprised me even though I'd read books by the same author, or even my first week of college, which did not go as planned. These surprises came because I had no insight; no one told me what to expect or what that experience might be like. Then sometimes I did have some insight before entering a new experience. I talked to a friend about a trip I was about to take; I read a review before starting a new book; I did some research about a new experience I was about to have, and my new trip, book, experience, person, or place was positively impacted by that knowledge and/or learning. No, I didn't have a crystal ball to help me look into the future, but I did have a better idea about what was going to happen. I was prepared and knowledgeable.

So often in our classrooms, we spend an enormous amount of time reteaching or remediating learning. Although we get some sense of satisfaction when students learn or master a concept, it also reminds us of those moments when we wish students had some prior knowledge or experience. Have you ever thought, "If only students had some time, experience, or knowledge *before* the teaching, they would have been much better prepared and ready for the new learning"?

When we think about preparing our students, we have the ability to positively impact student learning *before* a lesson through the power of pre-teaching.

According to Berg and Wehby (2013), pre-teaching is an effective methodology for students from elementary through high school.

> Preteaching may be presented as a whole-class, small-group, or one-on-one activity. It is recommended that grouping should be flexible

and responsive to student abilities and take into account both student needs in the current unit of study and performance in previous units (Munk et al., 2010). Selection of who needs preteaching may require targeted assessment or pretesting regarding content knowledge of the upcoming lesson or unit.

Pre-teaching is about teaching students *before* they encounter a lesson, concept, or new learning experience. Although there is a universal belief that activating schema and knowledge—preparing students for learning and building knowledge quickly and effectively—will benefit all learners, I seldom see pre-teaching used in classrooms. This is largely due to time constraints and the busy nature of today's classrooms. However, this simple teaching move has payoffs for students. Pre-teaching is proactive, and it removes the elements of cognitive and emotional disengagement. The key is to find ways to integrate pre-teaching into the framework and fabric of everyday instruction. This process will help us meet our strengths-based goals for learners, especially when we match the pre-teaching to the learner by identifying what she can do well and needs most.

#17   *Activate and Build Knowledge with an Updated KWL Chart (K–8)*

KWL charts are not new, but they are an effective and strategic tool for pre-teaching, especially in the new format I suggest. Pre-teaching with an updated KWL chart helps students "build the roadmap" for learning. It provides learners with a starting point and builds a bridge from what they don't know to what they need to know. You draw upon and review previous learning experiences, activate knowledge and related information, and provide experiences so the learner builds knowledge of the new topic. I recommend this kind of pre-teaching for learners whose biggest obstacle is activating (or using) background information and for learners whose greatest strength is bringing their schema to new learning.

Two elements lead to the successful use of an updated KWL chart. The first is that this KWL chart is worded differently. This minor shift in language, a bend on an oldie but goodie, helps students to think differently. Rather than *What Do I Know? What Do I Want to Know?* and *What I Learned?* ask *What Do I Know? What Do I Wonder,* and *What Do I Now Know?* Wondering is active and is based on student interest and curiosity. In addition, I have students answer the question, *What Do I Now Know?* often and at various points of the learning, not just at the end of the text, experience, or unit. Asking the newly worded question as the learning is happening allows the learner to make meaning over time.

The second difference is that students interact with the chart collaboratively. This collaboration serves a slightly different but important role in each of the questions. When I ask students to individually answer the first question—*What Do I Know?*—I often receive nothing. When I ask students to answer this question collaboratively, they generate a collective response that helps them make meaning and build schema. When I ask students the second question—*What Do I Wonder?*—they often build upon each other's wonderings, growing more interested and curious and asking more sophisticated questions. With the third question—*What Do I Now Know?*—students use their collective brainpower to make meaning. With an updated KWL chart, the goal is not to assess knowledge (although it can still serve that purpose) but to collaboratively build conceptual understanding and background knowledge.

I used the updated KWL chart in an eighth-grade humanities classroom when students were moving into book clubs. Each book club was going to read a book about World War II. One of the book clubs was about to read *Maus*. In their preliminary conversation, I noticed the readers had no historical context. They didn't understand the setting of the text, nor did they have much background knowledge about the World War II time period. I realized this lack of knowledge was going to negatively impact their comprehension and interaction with the text. I decided to pre-teach (not just for the two struggling readers in the group but for all of the learners) to activate prior knowledge and build new knowledge. We used a KWL chart that looked like this:

What Do I Know?	What Do I Wonder?	What Do I Now Know? (My Learning)

Before reading the text, students recorded what they knew collectively. The body of information they pulled together activated knowledge in some and built new knowledge in others. Then we listed what we wondered. We started on the site wonderopolis.org, but then moved to a classroom-generated platform (using Padlet, we asked students to post and respond to a wondering) that grew the knowledge they needed to effectively engage with the text.

We started adding to the *What Do I Now Know?* column right away, after reading and discussing the first part of the text. To complete this final column of the chart, students referred to their response and annotation work from the unit, thinking both about the setting (historical time period and location) and the evolution of the characters. We focused on the times when the setting impacted the text, as well as the times when the character came to a new conclusion, understanding, or insight about his life and the period in which he lived, to build our collective understanding of what we now know.

#18   *Pre-Teach So Students Can Pre-Learn (2–8)*

With pre-teach to pre-learn, the goal is to provide students with direct instruction and practice prior to a lesson. Quite often, one to two sessions of pre-teaching will provide students with the discrete skills, background, vocabulary, and conceptual understanding needed to be successful throughout an entire unit of study. We want to provide learners with information and experiences essential to the success of the upcoming lessons. This kind of pre-teaching can be implemented up to three days prior to new learning. Pre-teaching skills prior to a lesson or activity not only has a positive effect on skill development but also has a much more positive effect on student self-efficacy (Lalley and Miller 2006).

When you engage students in a pre-learning lesson, in essence, you preview, prime, and prepare them for the learning to come. I follow the same steps as a typical minilesson but with more checking for understanding, guided try-it practice, and tangible artifacts. I recommend this kind of pre-teaching for learners who struggle in a particular content area, learners who have been identified as in need of the particular skill or strategy being taught, and/or learners who need language support. In addition, learners who have a strength in learning with tangible artifacts benefit from this type of pre-teaching.

Before an upcoming unit on sedimentary and metamorphic rocks, I implemented a pre-learning lesson with James. See Figure 4.1 for a description of James's pre-learning lesson.

Consider using a digital platform to pre-teach. One such platform is Kahoot!. Kahoot! is a review and reinforcement tool, but you can also use it to introduce topics and concepts to students. A blind Kahoot! is used to introduce a concept to students rather than reinforce it. According to Kahoot.com, when using a blind Kahoot! to pre-teach, you carefully consider five to six questions you want students to answer. They should be questions *you know they don't know the answer to*. The first question or two serve as a mechanism for discussion and explanation/introduction of the concept, and the second and third questions reinforce that concept. The next two questions continue to reinforce that concept, but with a twist; the more questions they answer, the more information they accumulate. For example, a blind

LESSON STAGE	MOVES I MADE AS A TEACHER/ MOVES JAMES MADE AS A STUDENT	HOW THIS IS DIFFERENT FROM A TYPICAL LESSON
Before the Lesson	I invited James to a five-slide Google Slides presentation I was planning to use in my pre-teaching lesson. James looked at the slides.	Students do not typically view teaching materials before a lesson. Although it is not mandatory to view materials before a pre-teaching lesson, having students do so positively impacts them as it builds and activates their schema.
Warm-Up: Engage, Connect	James entered the pre-teaching session excited. He had viewed the slides (and decided on his own that he would watch a BrainPOP video prior to our session). I stated the goal of our time together was to explore the ways that sedimentary rocks are different from metamorphic rocks and learn how sedimentary rocks become metamorphic.	Students have more say. James shared his initial thinking and excitement over the materials he viewed prior to our session.
Teach	I used an organizer to show James how sedimentary rocks can change into metamorphic rocks (see Figure 4.2). James held each rock type and described the rocks in front of him. We discussed the vocabulary; I introduced him to the verb *metamorphose*.	Although I always recommend using tools to teach, I used both physical artifacts (rocks) and an organizer in this lesson. Advance organizers are created to meet the specific needs of a student. I created this one for pre-teaching this concept, anticipating potential points of confusion and difficulty. It highlighted the process, concept and key vocabulary.
Try: Engage Students in the Concept or Skill through Guided Practice	James asked questions, then viewed his BrainPOP video again. He stopped at a particular part to show me rocks forming. James asked questions regarding rock change—namely where in the earth rocks change and how heat and pressure affect the changes.	Guided practice should be a part of every lesson, but here students are quite active and hands on. Students often identify what is confusing, ask questions, and manipulate objects.
Clarify and Link	James talked through the rock cycle, naming the steps of change from sedimentary to metamorphic.	Students reiterate the learning rather than the teacher.

Figure 4.1: Pre-Learning Lesson with James (Third Grader)

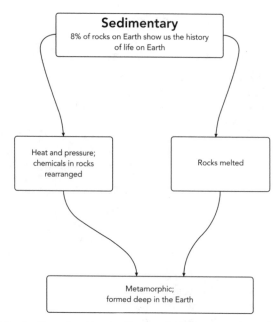

Figure 4.2: An Organizer Used to Pre-Teach Concepts and Vocabulary

Kahoot! used to teach the concept of the rock cycle to James and his peers might ask the following questions:

- What is metamorphosis?
- How do rocks change form?
- What is sediment?
- What is used to change sediment (or sedimentary rocks)?
- What kind of rocks do sedimentary rocks become?
- What does metamorphic mean?

After the teacher introduces the first two questions, students attempt to answer them. Again, students are *not* expected to be able to answer the questions correctly; this is considered a blind question, and the teacher uses the first two questions to teach/pre-teach. While students grapple with the content, attempting to formulate an answer, the teacher takes the opportunity to share information and content. The teacher then asks the next two questions. Students should be able to answer these next two questions as they reinforce the concept just taught. In between each question/set of questions, the teacher provides one to two minutes of instruction. Students are then asked to answer the last two questions. More information on using a blind Kahoot! as a pre-teaching tool can be found at www.getkahoot.com.

Incorporate Text Previewing and Introductions (K–8)

Text previewing and introductions—what I like to refer to as a warm-up session for reading—are a quick and efficient type of pre-teaching. Envision this as the stretching we do before exercise; however, here we are preparing our brains for learning! I use previewing when I want to increase reading engagement and make texts more accessible for particular learners.

Interacting with texts before a lesson or reading experience has huge payoff. A text introduction (similar to what might happen in a guided reading lesson) or text preview will provide students with information and experiences that will make the reading much more accessible.

For informational texts, you might:

- Read the back cover copy.
- Discuss the author, genre, and form.
- Read the table of contents.
- Pre-read text features, including photos, maps, and other graphic aids.
- Go to a particular section to pre-read the headings and captions.
- Ask specific questions students have and want answered in the text.

In essence, you show students how to navigate the text. Knowing how a particular text works makes information more accessible.

For narrative texts, you might:

- Read the back cover copy.
- Discuss the author.
- Name the setting.
- Read the chapter titles.
- Notice the length of each chapter.
- Unpack the structure of the text.
- Read an author's note or any other special page.

In either genre, you might choose to read aloud (short, key segments of text) or teach a few power words (words essential to the concept or new learning) to support pre-teaching. When handing the reins of pre-teaching over to students, I teach them the strategy of TAGS. The acronym TAGS is a condensed way to name the steps I take during a text introduction/preview. TAGS stands for:

T – Read the title. This includes any subtitles or chapter titles.

A – Consider the author. What do you know about this author, including what else she may have written or author credibility?

G – Consider the genre, including the features, form, and structure.

S – Activate schema. What do we know about this topic or theme?

In elementary classrooms, there are a few times in the day when teachers can pre-teach. One is at the beginning of the day or during the unpacking and "checking in" part of the morning. This is a time when the teacher is typically not bound by teaching or other duties and students can be independent. For middle school students, try the previewing pre-teaching strategy at the beginning of the period, perhaps during a quick collaborative task or "Do Now." Have a pre-teaching station set up in your room (or make the area of the room where you typically confer with students a pre-teaching spot) and conduct a five- to ten-minute preview in one-on-one or small-group conferences. Once routines for the year are set, this process is a great way to support struggling learners.

Middle school reader Lauren was a chronic "book abandoner." Abandoning a book is a common issue with many readers who lack stamina and ability to carry ideas within a text across any length of time or length of text. Lauren fit this profile precisely. She had not yet completed a whole book by the time I met her in the late fall. During reading time, I noticed that she looked up from her book every one or two minutes. In addition, Lauren had trouble discussing any text she was reading, whether an independent text, a core novel, or a short story within her book club.

My goal was to get her started on a book she could stick with. She decided that she wanted to read *Wonder* by R. J. Palacio. Lauren attempted to read *Wonder* earlier in the year but was not able to stick with it. She chose *Wonder* because she was attracted to the theme of the book and felt a connection with the character, Augie. She was also influenced by the fact that most of her peers had already read the book and highly recommended it. I knew that she was interested in reading the text but had to figure out how to make this book enjoyable and accessible for her.

I decided to focus on the book's interesting text structure. During our pre-teach conference, we previewed the text together and examined its structure. We talked about how the text is divided not only into chapters but also into parts. Each part begins with an epigraph and is narrated by a different character. I taught her how a reader needs to think about the epigraph before, during, and after reading the chapter. We also talked about ways she could navigate and manage the different narrators within the text. I asked Lauren to spend a few moments previewing the text, noticing the features I had introduced her to.

When I visited Lauren's classroom a few weeks later, I found a very different reader. She was focused, engaged, and almost done with *Wonder*. In fact, as soon as I entered the classroom, she was eager to share her thinking with me about what she had read since the last time I saw her. This confirmed for me how important and powerful previewing can be for a reader!

#20 Hook Students Through Authentic Digital Resources and Experiences (K–8)

If we can engage our students from the start, and provide them with information or experiences prior to a lesson (or at the beginning of a lesson or unit), we are setting up all our students for success. Hooking students into learning through an authentic resource or experience is another way to build a knowledge base and cultivate interest. This kind of pre-teaching may even be physically active and/or kinesthetic.

Just as a movie has a trailer (a short clip of film parts) to entice a potential viewer to go see the movie, our teaching can incorporate a hook to engage our struggling learners. In this type of pre-teaching, we use a hook—a video clip, meme, virtual reality, or kinesthetic activity—to entice the learner and introduce her to the concepts to come. This form of pre-teaching brings reluctant learners to the lesson in an interactive and engaging way; at the same time, students learn important concepts, vocabulary, or skills.

Seventh-grade math co-teachers Betsy Peterson and Marissa DePalma implemented this kind of pre-teaching in their classroom. Betsy and Marissa have a diverse array of learners, and pre-teaching concepts, vocabulary, and skills have been an important part of the instructional approach. Betsy and Marissa had an upcoming math unit on volume and surface area. While these concepts were introduced in previous grades, Betsy sometimes finds that some students don't retain the learning from previous years. To be successful in this unit, it is important to understand the definitions of volume and surface area, the concepts of filling vs. wrapping, and the reasons why these concepts are studied in mathematics.

Initially, Betsy and Marissa were going to teach the volume and surface area lessons and remediate or reteach as necessary. During our planning it became evident that pre-teaching some concepts would benefit many of the students in the class. We decided to hook students through a video clip about math in the real world.

Betsy and Marissa spent the first week of the unit implementing the first few lessons of the unit and gauging the background, interest, and understandings of the learners. We then used this information to plan for the next series of lessons, which included some pre-teaching. For our lesson on surface area, we started our whole class time with a video hook. Our hook was an authentic resource (#authres): a video illustrating volume and surface area of any shape. We chose this video: www.youtube.com/watch?v=SJGpKnI-784. Betsy and Marissa then moved into a parallel teaching model (see Chapter 10 for more information on co-teaching models). The students were divided by those who needed more pre-teaching and those who needed less. Marissa's group continued with a deeper explanation and exploration of the concepts presented in the hook. They reviewed concepts regarding various shapes and then interacted with objects that helped identify the difference between volume and surface area. Betsy's group moved on more quickly. They had a short debrief of the video, using that as a springboard to jump right into the lesson.

Although this hook was a digital resource, a kinesthetic activity can also benefit struggling learners. As a fourth-grade teacher, I integrated interactive activities and role playing as ways to pre-teach in a unit of study. At the beginning of our Revolutionary War study I planned a "tax day." Students were given a certain number of tokens. They had to submit tokens as a form of tax to participate in typical components of our classroom and day (sharpening a pencil, having snack, going to recess, going to the bathroom, using a classroom resource such as a laptop or book). As students gave me tokens, they interacted with the history and vocabulary (Pencil Sharpening "Act," "No taxation without representation," "Give me liberty [or my snack] or give me death") from the historical time period.

These powerful resources and experiences provide students with exposure, language, and understandings before a future lesson. See Figure 4.3 for some tips and resources if you want to try to hook students through digital experiences.

1. Go digital. Flip the pre-teaching by finding or creating two- to five-minute videos that can be viewed one to two days before a lesson. Post these pre-teaching clips to YouTube, Google Classroom, or even your class web page. You can create your own videos or use the enormous number of resources that are at our fingertips. Some of my favorites are:

- Khan Academy (www.khanacademy.org). Khan Academy has free, simple, student-friendly videos on an enormous array of disciplines and topics for students in grades 2–8.

- #Authres. This is a Twitter hashtag for authentic resources. Authentic resources are resources created or used to acquire language. They also enable learners to acquire vocabulary, concepts, and knowledge. #Authres can be videos, memes, and even virtual reality experiences and can be found on YouTube, Pinterest, and Twitter.

- BrainPOP. BrainPOP is a subscription site with animated movies, games, and other teaching tools across the disciplines. Although this is not free, it offers a tremendous number of resources that can be used for pre-teaching at school and at home.

2. Shift your definition of "extra help" time. Rather than always using extra help time as an opportunity to reteach and remediate learning, use this time to introduce new concepts. Doing so will positively shift your teaching to being more proactive and will encourage students to be more present and minds-on during lessons.

Figure 4.3: Tips for Using Digital Resources

Humanities (ELA and/or SS)

If you are pre-teaching with a text, provide students with markers, highlighters, and sticky notes to use as you interact with the text. Or, pre-mark the text so that only part of it is used in the pre-teaching. You can mark the features that will facilitate successful reading (headings, bold words, a particularly important sidebar) or mark parts of the text that will be the only parts students interact with during the pre-teaching. A third possibility is to pre-read some of the text with students so that they can stand on the shoulders of the previous read during the lesson.

Math

If you are pre-teaching a math concept, have manipulatives handy, such as coins, fraction pies, graph paper, or base-ten blocks. These tools will enable students to grapple with the new learning in ways that lead to greater "stickability."

Science

If you are pre-teaching science, bring an object, artifact, or lab element to the pre-teaching. Give students time to interact with and experience the object or artifact. Then layer in conversation and explicit information. If the artifacts are materials for a lab, consider allowing students a quick try-it with the lab. This pre-teaching, pre-learning can be a great scaffold for when they move to the lesson/lab.

Figure 4.4: Pre-Teaching Tool Suggestions Across Content Areas

KEEP IN MIND

When pre-teaching, tools matter. The Chinese proverb, "I hear and I forget, I see and I remember, I do and I understand," is true in pre-teaching. Use objects to ensure maximum student benefit. Tactile tools should be included in pre-teaching lessons whenever possible. Figure 4.4 shows some tool options across content areas.

Pre-teaching takes time, as does any type of differentiated instruction, yet the benefits for students are profound. Pre-teaching can help our most struggling students become confident. Teacher Justin Minkel (2015) shares, "For the same twenty-minute investment of time, we can change the way a child sees himself as a reader, thinker, or mathematician. We can give Manuel the rare experience of being the kid who gets it first, who helps the other kids figure it out, who is ready with the answer the moment he hears the question."

CHAPTER FIVE

Incorporate Small-Group Instruction

As classroom teachers, we are often asked to deliver additional support for struggling learners. Theoretically, we are in full agreement. In fact, we are often asked to implement "interventions" or supplemental support to struggling learners within the confines of the regular school day. Again, theoretically, we are in full agreement.

But then the questions arise. When? When can we do this? How? How can we do this? And, of course, where and what? Where will we do this, and what will everyone else be doing? Many years ago, I was dramatically influenced by Richard Allington's research, which stated that the frequency and intensity with which we support struggling learners would have a positive impact on their reading development (Allington 2005, Allington and Gabriel 2012). So once again, I was in full agreement that struggling learners needed more and that it would greatly impact their literacy development if I could provide more frequent and intense support.

The questions still remain. When? How? Where? What? The answers lie in small-group instruction. The key is to implement small-group instruction in ways that feel manageable and in ways that will support struggling learners best.

#21 *Decide on the Most Responsive Form of Small-Group Instruction (K–8)*

In today's teaching world, there are many different types, and thus many different definitions, of small-group instruction; this can be confusing. Over the past few years, I have thought a lot about what we have available to us as teachers of reading and writing, and have come up with a few clear and effective ways to instruct our struggling readers and writers.

TYPES OF SMALL-GROUP INSTRUCTION IN THE WRITING WORKSHOP

As a writer, I have benefitted from a variety of supports for my writing. And as a teacher of struggling writers, I too know the power of supporting learners in a small-group setting. The key is to envision what type of small-group instruction would work best for your learners and then implement that type of instruction during writing time. See Figure 5.1 for a chart of five powerful types of small-group writing instruction, including how to implement, what materials to use, and why these support struggling learners.

TYPES OF SMALL-GROUP INSTRUCTION IN THE READING WORKSHOP

What has been powerful for me as a teacher in general, but certainly as a teacher of struggling learners, is to utilize and stand on the shoulders of the collaborative teaching and learning structures available to me. When I think about the types of small-group instruction I can implement with readers, I consider the collaborative structures that already exist in the room and then layer them with the different ways readers might need support.

The outcome is Figure 5.2 below, which captures the myriad of ways I support readers in small groups. Each small-group instruction type utilizes the power that exists in that structure. The chart is organized as a gradual release, moving from more teacher-directed small-group instruction to more student-driven structures. Envision your role shifting from teacher, to reading partner/facilitator, to coach.

In each of the reading and writing small-group structures, two fundamental elements are present: readers and writers receive focused, needs-based, quick, relevant, and engaging instruction, *and* readers and writers spend the majority of the time reading, writing, and making meaning.

To decide who, what, and where for small-group instruction in either reading or writing, I recommend a simple three-step process:

1. Create/use a formative assessment(s) that will provide you with information about your students and enable you to create small groups.

2. Synthesize the information and create a checklist. This can be a basic grid with skills/strategies across the top and student names down the side. You can use a check or X, or a 1–3 scale. See Figure 5.3 for an example.

3. Use a small-group instruction planner(s) to envision the content, structure, and timing of the small-group instruction. Investigate any resources you have to find ideas, texts, and tools for small-group instruction.

TYPE OF SMALL-GROUP INSTRUCTION	EXPLANATION	LESSON STRUCTURE	MATERIALS USED
Strategy Lessons	Lessons in a particular skill or strategy. This can include strategies for generating ideas in writing, rehearsing writing, drafting writing, revising writing, the craft of writing, editing writing, and so on. You can pull strategy groups in two ways: • Form strategy groups using formative assessments and ongoing observation of student writing. Pull strategy groups during writing workshop instead of having a conference. • Create a strategy group based on a conference you just had. Ask yourself: Who else needs this instruction? Pull those writers into a small group.	• Warm-up • Teaching point • Try together • Students read and try in their own writing • Strategy application conversation • Connection to ongoing work	Model writing (teacher-generated, student-generated, anchor text) Student writing (in folder, notebook, or draft)

How does this type of small-group instruction support struggling writers?

Strategy lessons are the perfect blend of needs-based instruction and accessible, independent practice. Strategy lessons offer opportunities for teachers to focus on the specific strategies that writers need. Teachers provide instruction in the specific strategy and afford writers a forum to practice the strategy in their own writing.

Minilesson Do-Over	Some students benefit from a repeat of a recently taught minilesson in a small-group setting. The teaching point will remain the same, but vary the teaching technique. For example, if we looked at a published mentor text in the lesson, I may try to use student writing or conduct a shared writing in the small-group do-over.	• Warm-up • Teaching point • Try together • Students read and try in their own writing • Connection to ongoing work	Model writing (teacher-generated, student-generated, anchor text) Student writing (in folder, notebook, or draft)

How does this type of small-group instruction support struggling writers?

Minilesson do-overs are an excellent small-group option for struggling writers. Struggling learners benefit from re-teaching in a small-group setting, and minilesson do-overs are one practical way to do that. It is essential to vary the modeling method. Consider the type of model (teacher model, student model, published texts model, or shared writing) that would benefit this group of struggling learners most, and use this method of modeling in the do-over.

(continues)

Figure 5.1: Small-Group Writing Instruction

Figure 5.1: Small-Group Writing Instruction *(continued)*

TYPE OF SMALL-GROUP INSTRUCTION	EXPLANATION	LESSON STRUCTURE	MATERIALS USED
Minilesson Pre-Teach	Many struggling students benefit from pre-teaching. The goal is to teach a small group of students *before* the whole-class minilesson so that they have exposure and experience with a strategy/skill/concept beforehand.	• Warm-up • Teaching point • Try together • Students read and try in their own writing • Connection to ongoing work	Model writing (teacher-generated, student-generated, anchor text) Student writing (in folder, notebook, or draft)

How does this type of small-group instruction support struggling writers?

As educators, we know that pre-teaching is a valuable and valid method for supporting struggling learners; however, we seldom feel we can find the time to pre-teach. Here, pre-teaching happens whenever small-group instruction happens, and finding time is no longer an issue. Pre-teaching enables a struggling learner to come to future teaching with instruction and experience in a concept or skill. The struggling learner can then activate this schema during a future lesson and have a hook to hang his hat of new learning.

	EXPLANATION	LESSON STRUCTURE	MATERIALS USED
Read Like a Writer Craft Groups	Read like a writer craft groups are your opportunity to elevate the quality of student writing through an intense yet quick study of another writer. The purpose is to provide students with the opportunity to collaboratively study a mentor text and then find moves for their own writing. In many instances, I ask students to find a specific mentor sentence or part, copy that part on a sentence strip or in their writer's notebook, and use that part to mentor their own writing.	• Warm-up • Teach: Ask, what is this writer doing? Where can we try this in our own writing? • Try: Students try moves in their own writing. Find mentor parts. • Share and connect: Students share (as a group or in pairs) their try-its; Connect to ongoing work.	T-chart to document craft moves Anchor text(s) by an author Student writing: try-its, entries, or drafts

How does this type of small-group instruction support struggling writers?

Read like a writer craft groups stand on the shoulders of two key elements that support struggling learners: clear and explicit models and repeated practice. Finding mentor sentences or parts is also a tactile and tangible way to provide students with a model of good writing that they can emulate in their own work. In addition, the structure of the lesson builds in time for try-its and low-stakes practice at writing. This practice and feedback support a struggling learner's development.

(continues)

Figure 5.1: Small-Group Writing Instruction *(continued)*

TYPE OF SMALL-GROUP INSTRUCTION	EXPLANATION	LESSON STRUCTURE	MATERIALS USED
Peer Feedback Groups/ Workshopping Your Writing	During this type of small-group instruction, I bring students together to read their pieces and receive feedback. If we are workshopping one at a time, one writer will ask for suggestions based on a specific need or goal she has for her writing. The other writers give specific suggestions (a glow and a grow or compliment/ suggestion). The writer envisions using the strategy and commits to trying one strategy. If I am structuring this as partnership work, I will provide a quick demo and then have students turn to their partner to receive feedback. The same structure is used.	• Warm-up • Teach/demo • Student share • Peer feedback • Group reflection and conversation	Student writing Writing suggestions anchor chart Sticky notes to record glow/grow

How does this type of small-group instruction support struggling writers?

Workshopping writing is an incredibly powerful way to support a writer, and struggling writers benefit enormously from this practice. Why? The structure of the lesson is positive and active—each writer gives suggestions and receives suggestions and then has an opportunity to envision these changes in their writing. In addition, the lesson is structured as collaborative practice, and struggling learners benefit from the small-group or partnership structure.

TYPE OF SMALL-GROUP INSTRUCTION	EXPLANATION	LESSON STRUCTURE	MATERIALS USED
Guided Reading	The teacher guides students through the reading of a leveled text that is at the determined placement level. This is considered their highest instructional level and is typically one level above their independent reading level.	• Warm-up: Prior knowledge conversation, text introduction, picture walk/preview, vocabulary, set a purpose for reading • Students read • Teaching point • Comprehension conversation • Word work/follow-up (Optional)	Leveled books; works best if you use short texts or excerpts/parts from longer texts

How does this type of small-group instruction support struggling readers?

Guided reading, by nature and intent, is guided instruction and practice in texts that are at the reader's instructional level. Therefore, the instruction is at their zone of proximal development, providing readers with instruction and support for reading, while at the same time attending to accelerating reading growth. During a guided reading lesson, the teacher can support many aspects of the reading process, including decoding, fluency, comprehension, and writing about reading. Teachers can plan to support readers according to their specific reading goals within a level but will also pay close attention to the reading process and support readers with a teaching point after reading the text.

Strategy Lessons	The teacher gathers a group of students with the same needs, models how to use a specific skill or strategy, and facilitates support as students practice the strategy in their independent texts.	• Warm-up • Teaching point • Try together • Students read and try in their independent books • Connect to ongoing work	Model in a shared text (such as a previously read short text or class instructional read-aloud); students practice in their independent books.

How does this type of small-group instruction support struggling readers?

Strategy lessons are the perfect blend of needs-based instruction and accessible, independent practice. Strategy lessons offer opportunities for teachers to focus on the specific strategies that readers need. Teachers instruct readers in the specific strategy and give them a forum to practice the strategy in an independent-level text. Readers have the added bonus of being with other readers who are doing the same work.

(continues)

Figure 5.2: Small-Group Reading Instruction

Figure 5.2: Small-Group Reading Instruction *(continured)*

TYPE OF SMALL-GROUP INSTRUCTION	EXPLANATION	LESSON STRUCTURE	MATERIALS USED
Literacy Centers	Students in grades K–1 work collaboratively, practicing literacy skills and habits (through playing, reading, writing, talking, learning). Teacher leans in to support students in a center, modeling and supporting readers.	• Research/observe students • Warm-up/connection • Teaching point/support • Try together • Students continue work in center	Variety of materials

How does this type of small-group instruction support struggling readers?
Another small-group structure that can be of enormous support to struggling learners is the literacy center. When done well, centers provide students with opportunities to practice various elements of reading, writing, speaking, and listening with collaborative support.

Small Group Shared Reading	Teacher and students collaboratively read a shared text over 3-5 sessions	Day 1: Introduction, First Read Day 2: Phonics/Word Study, Second Read Day 3: Fluency, Third Read Day 4: Comprehension, Fourth Read Day 5: Comprehension and Celebration	Variety of Materials

How does this type of small group instruction support struggling readers?
Shared reading is a collaborative reading construct that supports fluency, accuracy, and comprehension of texts in a supportive setting. During shared reading, readers benefit from the text choice (engaging texts at the instructional level) and the support of collaborative reading and thinking. In small group shared reading, the teacher can model accuracy, fluency, and phrasing in ways that are meaningful and connected to this particular group of readers through choral, or echo reading, and comprehension through think aloud modeling and collaborative talk. Rereading a text is backed by research as a structure that builds fluency and comprehension in readers.

(continues)

Figure 5.2: Small-Group Reading Instruction *(continued)*

TYPE OF SMALL-GROUP INSTRUCTION	EXPLANATION	LESSON STRUCTURE	MATERIALS USED

Reading Clubs	Student-centered small-group reading. Students/partnerships meet with baskets of books for one or two weeks to read and talk about the books. The teacher leans into the club and coaches the students.	• Research/observe students.
		• Teacher coaches into the club/conversation.
		  • Warm-up/connection
		  • Teaching point/support
		  • Try together
		  • Students continue to read and talk as a club.
			Books from various authors and genres. Clubs can be based on a series, character, genre, or nonfiction topic (e.g., transportation club, ocean animals club, WW II club, etc.)

Book Clubs	Student-centered small-group reading of a **shared**, student-chosen text. The teacher leans into the club and coaches the students.	• Research/observe students.
		• Teacher coaches into the club/conversation.
		  • Warm-up/connection
		  • Teaching point/support
		  • Try together
		  • Students continue to read and talk as a club.
			Short texts and chapter books at students' independent reading level

How does this type of small-group instruction support struggling readers?

Reading and book clubs are student-driven small-group reading collaborations. However, they are also opportunities for teachers to instruct in small groups. If students are in reading and book clubs, rather than implementing guided reading or strategy lessons, envision supporting readers in their club. Supporting struggling readers in this context enables teachers to support reading, writing, speaking, and listening skills. In addition, teachers can coach struggling readers in their collaborations and can utilize the collaborative structure to push thinking and deepen conversation.

Student	Topic: Chooses a topic that represents an issue they care about.	Lead: Hooks the reader and draws them into the writing.	Organization: Groups info and related ideas together.	Transitions: Writing flows from idea to idea with transition words that connect, compare, or show example.	Conclusion: Strong ending that is clear and persuasive; inspires the reader as a call to action.	Craft: Word choice and tone are persuasive and engaging.
Nolani	2	1	2	2	2	1
Jeff	2	2	3	1	2	1
Ethan	1	2	2	2	3	2
Kayley	2	1	2	2	2	3
Ben	3	3	1	2	2	2

Strategy Group: Nolani, Ethan, and Kayley in strategy lesson on organization. Use persuasive mentor text on dangerous sports as model.

Read Like a Writer Craft Group: Nolani, Jeff, Ethan, and Ben in craft group on conclusions. Focus on endings that inspire readers to take action. Use Jack's student writing and Malala's speech.

1= **Not Yet!**

2= **Approximating or Approaching**

3= **Implementing in Writing**

Figure 5.3: Checklist to Determine Small-Group Instruction

#22 *Implement Teaching Intensives (K–8)*

One way to powerfully implement small-group instruction is to embody the belief that you, as a classroom teacher, can positively impact struggling learners during the time you have available with them during the school day. I call this implementing teaching intensives, and I do this for different learners at different times.

What do I mean by implementing a teaching intensive? A teaching intensive is a focused period of time (say two to four weeks) where *in the course* of my daily literacy instruction I meet with struggling learners more frequently.

How is this done? I consider the following:

- Teaching intensives are possible in classrooms where differentiation occurs. If you are using differentiated structures such as the Daily Five (Boushey and Moser 2006), literacy or content area centers, or a workshop approach to teaching, you differentiate. "[Interventions] must include flexible grouping that allows teachers to target instructional needs and adjust instruction within and beyond the general curriculum. This includes a variety of homogeneous and heterogeneous small-group experiences, such as carefully organized day-to-day guided reading, student conferences, and side-by-side activities" (Howard 2009, 16). Generally, with a workshop approach to teaching, for every fifty- to sixty-minute period, students spend about thirty of those minutes in differentiated practice. A workshop structure should look like this:

  - ➤ Ten- to fifteen-minute minilesson
  - ➤ Thirty to forty minutes for independent practice (actually reading, writing, or working on differentiated math practice)
  - ➤ Five- to ten-minute wrap-up

- Plan for differentiated instruction during student independent practice time. This support is based on the definition of equity, which means that everyone gets what he needs, not the exact same thing. After a whole-class minilesson, I meet with students in differentiated teaching formats, either small-group instruction or conferences. The differentiated format can vary (see Figures 5.1 and 5.2 for examples), and the frequency can vary (in my eight-day cycle I see some learners once, some three times). I will see each learner at least once.

- Meet with struggling learners more frequently. I know that I have various options for how I can support them (small groups, individual conferences, center time), and I plan wisely. I strongly suggest you keep the same teaching point for

Classic Model of Instruction

MONDAY	TUESDAY	WEDNESDAY	THURSDAY	FRIDAY
	SGI or conference			SGI or conference

In this scenario, I will see each learner once or twice a week in a small-group lesson or individual conference per discipline (reading, writing, math).

Intensive Model 1a: Moderate Support

MONDAY	TUESDAY	WEDNESDAY	THURSDAY	FRIDAY
SGI	Check-in conference		Check-in conference	

In this scenario, I will see a struggling learner three times—once in a small-group lesson and two more times in check-in conferences.

Intensive Model 1b: Moderate Support

MONDAY	TUESDAY	WEDNESDAY	THURSDAY	FRIDAY
SGI	Reinforce same teaching point via another SGI or conference.		Reinforce same teaching point via another SGI or conference.	

In this scenario, also considered to be of moderate support, I will also see a struggling learner three times—once in a small-group lesson and then two additional times, either in another small-group lesson or in a conference, reinforcing the same teaching point.

Intensive Model 2a: Intensive Support

MONDAY	TUESDAY	WEDNESDAY	THURSDAY	FRIDAY
SGI	Check-in conference	SGI	Check-in conference	SGI or nothing

In this scenario, I am offering intensive support either four or five days a week. I might vary how I see this learner, balancing small-group lessons with conferences and shorter check-in conferences, but the idea is that I am ramping up the intensity or frequency of teaching.

Intensive Model 2b: Intensive Support

MONDAY	TUESDAY	WEDNESDAY	THURSDAY	FRIDAY
SGI	Reinforce same teaching point in various ways via SGI or conference.			

In this scenario, I am also offering intensive support for a struggling learner and am making the conscious decision to stick to the same teaching point each day in either another small-group lesson or in a conference.

Figure 5.4: Progression of Support for Students

more than one lesson. Popcorning around to different teaching points is not as effective as sticking with the same teaching point. With struggling learners, it is important to do something different to support them. Figure 5.4 is an example of how often I might offer a struggling learner support across one week.

How to have a check-in conference:

- Saddle up to the reader.

- Ask the reader how the "work" is going. This "work" is the specific teaching point from a previous SGI lesson or conference.

- Look for evidence of the work (a sticky note, quick description from the reader, asking the reader to read a page to you).

- Reinforce the teaching point, adjusting the practice the reader is doing, as necessary.

What might a teaching intensive look like? During our last coaching session, second-grade teachers Janine Grosso and Talysa Glogower asked me to model a reading strategy lesson that involved character work. We brainstormed and landed on a strategy lesson on how to deeply understand our characters by noticing what the characters say and do.

As I was teaching the lesson, we realized that two readers, Tommy and Giselle, were not quite ready for this level of reading work. They were still having trouble describing their characters; they needed additional support.

After the lesson, we brainstormed a plan for Giselle.

MONDAY	TUESDAY	WEDNESDAY	THURSDAY	FRIDAY
SGI	Reinforce same teaching point with another SGI or conference.		Reinforce same teaching point with another SGI or conference.	
(This was the strategy lesson I taught.)	(Janine would meet with Giselle in a conference, teaching her how to have a hunch about her character and read for evidence.)		(Janine would meet with Giselle in a guided reading lesson where the teaching point was all about getting to know characters and reading to find evidence.)	

Figure 5.5: Weekly Teaching-Intensive Plan for Giselle

The plan in Figure 5.5 felt manageable to Janine. She would follow up with Giselle, and a conference seemed like the best form of support. During an individual conference, Janine would reteach the strategy, and Giselle could apply the strategy to the characters in her independent book. In addition, Janine felt that it was good timing to meet with other readers at Giselle's level (in a guided reading lesson) and that reinforcing the same teaching point would be just as helpful for them. Figure 5.6 shows the plan we brainstormed for Tommy.

MONDAY	TUESDAY	WEDNESDAY	THURSDAY	FRIDAY
SGI	Check-in conference	SGI	Check-in conference	SGI
(This was the strategy lesson I taught.)	(Quick check-in to see if he has a hunch about his character.)	(Talysa would reinforce the strategy lesson character work with other readers who continue to need this work.)	(Quick check-in to see if he is tracking evidence of his hunch about his character.)	(Talysa would continue the strategy lesson character work with other readers who continue to need this work.)

Figure 5.6: Weekly Teaching-Intensive Plan for Tommy

Talysa would follow up with Tommy in his independent book (quickly and frequently so they could talk more specifically about his character and get him reading for evidence). In addition, Talysa also wanted to reinforce the character work strategy lesson with other readers who needed this teaching point. I also suggested that Tommy and his reading partner either read the same book (same book partnership) or swap their books. That way, Tommy's partner could provide additional support to understand characters, develop hunches, and find evidence through action and dialogue.

#23 *Use Planners to Manage Instruction (K–8)*

In all aspects of life, having a plan will help you implement small-group instruction in powerful, proactive, and manageable ways. Over the years, I have experimented with various types of small-group instruction planning forms that achieve

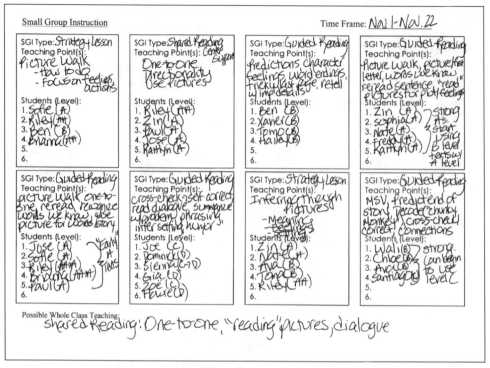

Figure 5.7: Sample Three-Week Small-Group Instruction Reading Planner: Kindergarten

different purposes. I use a content planner to manage the content and type of instruction, and, in conjunction, I use a timing planner to manage the timing and frequency of small-group instruction.

CONTENT PLANNERS

Utilize a planner that allows you to see the content and type of small-group instruction across a reasonable time period (such as a month). This planner records what you will teach, in what instructional context, and to whom. This planner provides a "class at a glance" view of your instruction but is specific and captures students, small-group instruction types, and teaching points. It provides a road map for managing the content and type of small-group instruction. See Figure 5.7 as an example.

Recently, fifth-grade teacher Meaghan Arias and I set out to do some planning for small-group instruction in reading. We decided to use a planner for strategy lessons. We wanted to identify whether any of these small-group strategy lessons would be pre-taught before the unit lessons. Meaghan's class was just entering a reading unit of study in Analyzing Character and Theme in Coming of Age

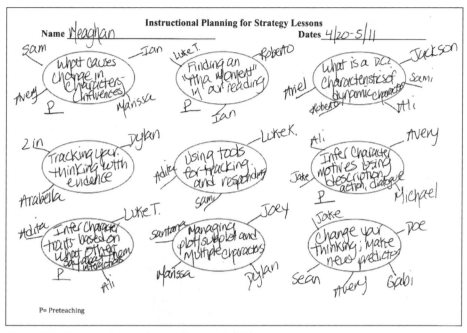

Figure 5.8: Meaghan's Instructional Planner, Grade 5

Novels. Meaghan was using *Wonder* by R. J. Palacio as the instructional read-aloud, and each student was reading his or her own coming of age novels. When Meaghan and I sat down to plan, we thought about her upcoming teaching, her readers, and what particular strategies and skills might cause difficulty for some of her students.

We used my strategy lessons instructional planner. She jotted teaching points that are connected both to her students and their needs and to the upcoming unit of study (see Figure 5.8). Some of the teaching points on Meaghan's planner are skills and strategies that some of her readers need now, either because they are not using these strategies or because they will need these strategies as their reading progresses (e.g., using tools for tracking, managing plot and subplot, changing your thinking by making new predictions). Other teaching points are related to upcoming whole-class minilessons (identifying and finding the influences that cause character change, finding "aha moments" in reading, and inferring character motives to name a few), and Meaghan and I felt these teaching points were going to be a challenge for some of the readers. Therefore, Meaghan decided that her next few strategy lessons would be devoted to pre-teaching these strategies and skills. Notice how those strategies have a "P" under the oval that identifies that these lessons will be pre-taught before the whole-class minilesson.

PLANNERS THAT MANAGE TIMING AND FREQUENCY

In conjunction with one of the other planners, I also suggest you use a planner that will enable you to manage the frequency and timing of your differentiated teaching across a one- to two-week period. This will allow you to determine when you will implement the lessons from your SGI content planner, balance small-group instruction and conferences, and implement more frequent instruction for your struggling learners. See Figure 5.9 as an example of a planner used to capture timing and frequency. It can be used for any discipline/workshop (reading, writing, math) to help you plan for a balance of small-group instruction and conferences. In addition, you can easily plan for and see the frequency with which you will meet with your struggling learners within the week.

INSTRUCTIONAL PLANNING: Conferences and Small-Group Instruction

	DAY 1	DAY 2	DAY 3	DAY 4	DAY 5
Reading Workshop					
Conferences					
Small-Group Instruction					
	DAY 6	DAY 7	DAY 8	DAY 9	DAY 10
Conferences					
Small-Group Instruction					
Total Number of Conferences: Total Number of Small-Group Lessons:					

Figure 5.9: Blank Small-Group Instruction and Conferences Timing and Frequency Planner

Two Week Instructional Planner: Conferences and Small Group Instruction

	Day 1	Day 2	Day 3	Day 4	Day 5
Reading Workshop					
Conferences	Tameka Nali Michael	Tommy ✓ Peyton Christina Natalie Zoe Giselle	Jackson Ben	Tommy ✓ Maggie ✓	
Small Group Instruction	Character (say/do) Tommy Giselle Kevin Devlin		Character Tommy Zoe Ethan Perry Megan	Level M	Tommy Brin Jackson Level L → Character/reactions	

	Day 6	Day 7	Day 8	Day 9	Day 10
Conferences	Seth Brian Ben		Brin Perry Ethan Giselle Peyton Christina		Megan Kevin Jackson Perry Michael Zoe
Small Group Instruction	Level N	level K		level K	

√ = Quick Check in

Figure 5.10: Sample of Timing and Frequency Planner

#24 Make Small-Group Instruction Matter: Ask, What Is Getting in the Learner's Way? (K–8)

Another important element of successful small-group instruction is the idea that the best outcomes are a result of targeted and specific instruction. This requires us to ask: What is getting in the learner's way? Then, we plan the instruction around this specific answer.

When it comes to providing specific and targeted support for struggling readers, begin with the question: *What is getting in the reader's way?* Often the answer falls into one of three categories—decoding/fluency, vocabulary, and comprehension. Each category is HUGE, so then you can ask the question again, but this time within the specific category: *What, with regard to vocabulary, is getting in the reader's way?* Consider the fact that strong readers need the following:

- Skills/strategies: things readers need to do in order to read accurately and make meaning
- Habits and dispositions: ways of thinking and working that make the reading process successful
- Concepts: background knowledge and ideas

Keeping in mind that strong readers need skills and strategies, habits and dispositions, and concepts, set out to create your intervention plan. Once you know what is getting in the reader's way, you can plan targeted instruction and practice, using appropriate and applicable tools. Figures 5.11–14 are charts that can help you make decisions about what strategies you will teach, as well as what tools you might use.

WHAT IS GETTING IN THE READER'S WAY?	WHAT STRATEGY, PRACTICE, OR TOOL CAN HELP?
Reading Engagement and Motivation	**Survey the reader.** Investigate the reader's preferences for genre, topic, and author, as well as general preferences around reading. For example, if the reader does better with texts that have short or episodic chapters, or enjoys texts with a strong female main character, help this reader to find those kinds of books to read.
	Develop stamina. Readers who are lacking in reading stamina can lose interest and motivation in a text. Therefore, build reading stamina by developing both the number of minutes a reader can attend to a text, as well as the number of pages he or she can read at one time. Begin by investigating the reader's pacing (Figure 6.1 can be used to find the number of minutes a reader can read) and build upon this. Have the reader set a goal to read for a few more minutes each time he or she reads, or allow the reader to read a few different texts in order to keep going.
	Offer collaboration opportunities. Reading partnerships and clubs are a great way to keep reading engagement high! Readers can plan reading or predict before they read, can read important parts or interesting scenes with dialogue during reading, or can retell, discuss the characters, and share opinions after reading. Collaborations keep a reader on track and engaged in reading!

Figure 5.11: Interventions for Reading Engagement and Motivation

WHAT IS GETTING IN THE READER'S WAY?	WHAT STRATEGY, PRACTICE, OR TOOL CAN HELP?
Accuracy and Fluency	**Use repeated readings.** Asking a reader to read the same text, with guidance and support (aided readings), can build accuracy and fluency. Readers can do repeated readings with shared reading texts (big books, poems, short articles, songs) and read independently and collaboratively.
	Consider text choice. Research shows us that it is best to use texts that struggling readers can read with at least 98 percent accuracy and strong comprehension for both independent *and* instructional reading (Allington and Gabriel 2012; Ehri, Dreyer, Flugman, and Gross 2007).
	Utilize echo reading and team reading in guided reading lessons. Using this practice for just a few pages can provide struggling readers with good models and guided practice in building accuracy and fluency.
	Practice reading with automaticity. Provide structures to practice sight words. My two favorites are:
	Establish a shared practice at the beginning of guided reading. Students come to the guided reading table and review sounds, letters, and or words collaboratively or independently as I settle the room or check in with other readers.
	Establish sight word practice as a part of their independent practice during reading time. Similarly, I provide readers with sight word cards (written in red, as instructors do when using the Orton-Gillingham approach—the color red is a higher visual cue) and ask that they start the independent reading or center time by reading and reviewing sight words for three to five minutes.

Figure 5.12 Interventions for Accuracy and Fluency

WHAT IS GETTING IN THE READER'S WAY?	WHAT STRATEGY, PRACTICE, OR TOOL CAN HELP?
Comprehension	**Instruct at the zone of actual development:** Think carefully about text level and level of instruction. This may mean that you decide a reader's placement level (Fountas and Pinnell 1996) for instructional reading is the same as his independent level.
	Tap into reader interest to increase motivation and progress. No doubt about it, readers are most successful when they are interested and engaged in the text. Therefore, frequently consider topic and genre interests when choosing texts for small-group instruction. In addition, always allow a reader to choose his or her independent texts based on experiences, interests, and comfort level.

Figure 5.13: Interventions for Comprehension

(continues)

Figure 5.13 (*continued*)

WHAT IS GETTING IN THE READER'S WAY?	WHAT STRATEGY, PRACTICE, OR TOOL CAN HELP?
Comprehension	**Model *think-aloud*.** *Think-aloud* is an instructional strategy that teachers frequently use to demonstrate the mind work of a proficient reader (themselves) during an instructional read-aloud. I *also* recommend this as a strategy that *readers can use* to monitor and develop comprehension. Determine parts of a reader's independent reading text at places where you want the reader to share their thinking. Mark those places with a sticky note. Provide the reader with a way to "think aloud" and demonstrate their comprehension. This can be through a partner conversation, by asking the reader to quickly jot thinking on a sticky note, or by using a technology tool such as VoiceThread (see Chapter 7 for more information). Ask the reader to think aloud, share ideas, and record thinking. Follow up in a reading conference to explore what the reader was thinking and what he could be thinking during those parts. **Establish and use collaborations.** Collaborations support the development of comprehension, there is no doubt about it. In *Every Child, Every Day* Allington and Gabriel write, "Time for students to talk about their reading and writing is perhaps one of the most underused, yet easy-to-implement, elements of instruction…Yet it provides measurable benefits in comprehension, motivation, and even language competence" (2012). Although I believe that readers can talk about any text, asking partners to discuss the same text (same-book partnerships) or the same text after your partner has read it (swap-book partnerships) will support comprehension development as readers discuss and make meaning together. **Scaffold with series books.** Encourage struggling readers to read multiple books in a series as their independent reading texts. Readers can rely upon their knowledge of key elements (predictable characters, settings, text structures, and book features) as a scaffold to their reading. With series books, students can read long and strong! **Provide text introductions.** One of my favorite (and honestly simplest) comprehension supports is to provide a reader with a text introduction before reading a text. This would look very similar to what you would do in a guided reading lesson. However, here you are introducing any text (an instructional read-aloud, book club book, independent book). Be sure to share any pertinent information about the genre, author, setting, plot, characters, or vocabulary, but don't overdo it. Give the reader enough to support comprehension, but still leave them with work to do to make meaning.

(*continues*)

Figure 5.13 *(continued)*

WHAT IS GETTING IN THE READER'S WAY?	WHAT STRATEGY, PRACTICE, OR TOOL CAN HELP?
Comprehension	**Ask, *What is this mostly about?*** A great and simple comprehension strategy for struggling readers is to ask themselves the question: *What is this mostly about?* When using this strategy, I usually mark students' text with a sticky note every few pages (as many pages as I feel they can read without stopping). As they get to each note, they ask themselves the question, what is this mostly about? They can then retell to a partner, retell to themselves using one of our summarizing strategies (tell it across five fingers, retell using story elements, or use the strategy of retelling through: *somebody, wanted, but, so* [Beers 2002]). If they can tell what that part of the text is mostly about, they read on. If not, they reread all or part of the text. **Talk to the author.** *What is the author trying to tell me?* This strategy is very similar to the strategy above, but here, readers consider the stopping point to be a conversation with the author. Therefore, the question is: *What is the author trying to tell me?* Once again, I mark parts of a reader's independent reading text, asking them to stop at each sticky note to ask themselves the question: *What is the author trying to tell me?* By focusing on this question, readers think about both big ideas and small details and make meaning as they consider reading as a transaction between the writer and the reader.

WHAT IS GETTING IN THE READER'S WAY?	WHAT STRATEGY, PRACTICE, OR TOOL CAN HELP?
Vocabulary: Teach tangible strategies for independent word solving.	**Teach *stop and think:*** Ask, *What does this word remind me of? Do I know any part of this word?* This is a simple vocabulary strategy that enables readers to have what I like to call word power. By analyzing words from an etymological perspective, we not only figure out words but do so in a way that helps us to retain the word and use the information when reading other words. **Teach students to return to the word to *read/reread around the word.*** This is a practical vocabulary strategy that enables a reader to use context to determine unknown words. The reader may read the word and continue to the end of the sentence to see if she can figure out the meaning of the unknown word. In addition, the reader can read a few sentences back and a few sentences forward to determine the meaning. This strategy is quite effective because it works for determining an unknown word most of the time!

Figure 5.14: Interventions for Vocabulary *(continues)*

Figure 5.14   *(continued)*

WHAT IS GETTING IN THE READER'S WAY?	WHAT STRATEGY, PRACTICE, OR TOOL CAN HELP?
Vocabulary: Teach tangible strategies for independent word solving.	**Use new vocabulary words in partner conversation.** Take words learned via the above-named strategies (*Stop and Think About Word Parts* or *Read/Reread Around the Word*), and use them in partnership conversation. Students love this word-building technique as it makes them feel sophisticated and smart. When reading, I ask them to jot words they are learning on a sticky note kept at the back of their independent book. This should be a quick jot so as not to interrupt the flow of reading. When they get together with their independent reading partner, they use the words in conversation. This solidifies their understanding and brings their word knowledge to the application level.
	Introduce important tricky vocabulary, focusing on the word parts. Provide the reader with a book introduction for their independent reading book, and introduce any key vocabulary that you think will be essential. This strategy allows the teacher to guide and scaffold vocabulary development. At the same time, it makes the student an active reader. It works especially well when you ask the reader to record the words on a sticky note and quickly look for them in context when reading.

#25 Record Keeping That Is Simple, Succinct, and Specific (K–8)

When it comes to record keeping, keep the three Ss—simple, succinct, and specific—in mind. I have experimented with various types of record-keeping tools for many years, and feel that in many ways, a record-keeping form and a system for keeping track of the forms is a personal choice, kind of like choosing a pair of shoes or a purse that fits your style and purpose. That said, when teachers ask me what record-keeping forms and system work best, my answer is always "The one that you will actually use!" The forms that I use are simple to use and enable me to be succinct and specific in the writing.

Figure 5.15 is one example of a record keeping tool that I used to take notes during small group instruction and conferences. In Figure 5.16, I show another form, this one a filled out example of my record keeping. Notice that in my notes I am trying to be succinct and specific, noting only what I need to in order to document and remember the following: the gist of the work, my teaching point, and evidence of strategies and goals. Figure 5.17a includes specific instructions on how to administer a running record comprehension check, and Figure 5.17b is an example of a generic running record form. It has space to take a running record

Level Q (DRA 40)

Student: _____

Book Title(s)/Level: _____

CONFERRING/SMALL-GROUP INSTRUCTION NOTES

DATE	NOTES	BEHAVIORS, SKILLS, AND POSSIBLE TEACHING POINTS
		Demonstrates ability and interest in reading a variety of texts across many genres (mystery, fantasy, historical fiction, realistic fiction, biography).
		Chooses books according to interest and purpose; has preferences and identity as a reader.
		Reads orally with fluency, expression, and phrasing.
		Actively acquires new vocabulary through reading.
		Adjusts reading pacing according to genre, purpose, and readability; can skim and scan.
		Shows the ability to summarize and demonstrates understanding of the text in writing. Summaries are organized. Stops to summarize at important points in longer texts.
		Uses text features such as illustrations, diagrams, and other graphic aides to help analyze text meaning.
		Sustains attention to text read over many days, remembering details and revising interpretations as new events occur.
		Goes beyond the text to infer and interpret characters' thoughts, feelings, motivations, and text themes.
Observations/Possible Future Teaching:		Compares the text with other books in an analytical way.
		Can follow a line of thought in conversations.
		Rereads texts to find evidence and support interpretive response.

© 2018 by Patricia Vitale-Reilly from *Supporting Struggling Learners*. Portsmouth, NH: Heinemann.

Figure 5.15: Record-Keeping Tool with Examples of Behaviors and Teaching Points (page one, including formulas for self correction and accuracy, or page three—more space for the running record) and on page two, has questions and prompts you can use to determine comprehension.

Reading Conference and Small Group Record Keeping Form

Name Ryan

Date:	Content:	Evidence of Strategies/Goals:
10/28	Reading going? Okay. What choosing? "N.F. chapter books." Did not understand genre	Goal: stamina: sticking to reading/keep focus
T.P.	Text genre intro → parts, narrative structure, use story to read	
11/10	Now reading Wayside book. Likes it. Retelling-unclear some events struggled. Not holding	Finished N.F. book!
T.P.	onto story. Post-it chunks → jot word, retell, use word to retell to partner	
11/14	strategy lesson: Holding onto story!: mini deadlines,	
T.P.	frequent self-retelling	
11/18	Abandoned book - F harder to navigate than N.F. Created short stack (N.F → F) to read → interest so can stick to	Abandoned Wayside book
11/20	Strategy lesson!: Using genre features to make meaning. Post-its good connecting to texts!	sticking to N.F. from short stack!

Possible Future Instruction:

- Using interests to drive reading
- Holding onto story/text (longer chunks)
- Lingering too long on a post-it (whole class)

Figure 5.16: Sample of Record Keeping Tool with Column for Evidence of Goals

RUNNING RECORD COMPREHENSION CHECK INSTRUCTIONS

Purpose: This assessment provides teachers with an opportunity to document and gauge oral reading, fluency, and comprehension of any reader, at any time, in any text.

Text: Record the title of text.

Level: Record the level of text.

Text Features: Record any remarkable text features that may impact the readability of the text. Possibilities include: a pattern within the text, extended dialogue, nonfiction text features, subject-specific vocabulary, etc. Leave blank if no remarkable text features are present.

Record of Oral Reading: Use the blank space provided to take a running record. A running record can be taken on page 1 of the assessment, or if more space is needed, on page 3. If page 3 is used, only use the top (text, level, and text features) and bottom (fluency, scores for accuracy and self-correction) of page 1.

Marking the Running Record Form

Record according to the following:

- Record a check for each accurately read word.
- Errors (E)—An error is recorded whenever a reader does any of the following:
  - ➤ Substitutes another word for a word in the text
  - ➤ Omits a word
  - ➤ Inserts a word
  - ➤ Has to be told a word.
- Draw a line above any word read incorrectly (an error). If the reader substitutes a word, write this substitution above the word. If the reader omits the word, record a dash.
- Self-corrections (SC)—Self-correction occurs when a reader realizes her or his error and corrects it. When a reader makes a self-correction, the previous miscue is not scored as an error, but scored as a self-correction. Mark an SC next to the word/substitution if the reader self-corrects.
- When making errors, or when self-correcting, a reader uses one or more cueing systems. Record:
  - ➤ *An (M) if the reader uses meaning*—Meaning is the cueing system in which the child takes her cue from meaning—what makes sense from thinking about the story background, information from pictures, or the meaning of a sentence. These cues assist in the reading of a word or phrase.
  - ➤ *An (S) if the reader uses structure*—Structure refers to the composition of language and is often referred to as syntax. Implicit knowledge of structure helps the reader to know if what she or he reads sounds correct.
  - ➤ *A (V) if the reader uses visual cues*—Visual information is related to the look of the letters in a word, the corresponding sound(s) a letter makes, and the word itself. A reader uses visual information when she studies the beginning sound, word length, familiar word chunks, and so forth.

Figure 5.17a: Running Record Comprehension Check Instructions *(continues)*

Figure 5.17a   *(continued)*

Accuracy Rate: Accuracy is expressed as a percentage. You can calculate the accuracy rate using the following formula: *total words read—total errors/total words read × 100 = accuracy rate.*

Self-Correction Rate: Self-correction rate is expressed as a ratio and is calculated by using the following formula: *number of errors + number of self-corrections/number of self-corrections = self-correction rate.* A proficient reader has a 1:2 self-correction rate, however, a self-correction rate of 1:2-1:5 is considered an acceptable rate.

Fluency

Note and record observations of:

- **Rate:** Does the reader move at a pace that is not too fast and not too slow?
- **Expression and Intonation:** Does the reader vary her voice according to punctuation and meaning of the text?
- **Phrasing:** Does the reader group words together in a smooth and consistent way?

Comprehension and Depth of Understanding

Page 2 of the Running Record Comprehension Check is a comprehension guide that will allow you to gauge a reader's depth of understanding. Follow the directions on the top of the page and record what the reader says. Ask general prompts if necessary.

Analyzing the Information from the Running Record Comprehension Check

Analyze the information gleaned from the reader. Consider the following:

	LEVELS A-K	LEVELS L-Z
Independent Level	95-100% accuracy; scores at least 9 points on the comprehension part	98-100% accuracy; scores at least 9 points on the comprehension part
Instructional Level	90-94% accuracy; scores at least 7 points on the comprehension part	95-97% accuracy; scores at least 7 points on the comprehension part

Note the reader's strengths. Consider instructing the reader in a conference or a small group if you notice the reader needs work with oral reading or fluency, or if the reader scored a 1 or a 2 on any portion of the comprehension section.

Name_____	Date_____	

Text:	Level:	
Text Features:		

Record of Oral Reading	**Error** Meaning Syntax Visual	**Self Correction** Meaning Syntax Visual

Note on Fluency (Pacing, Pausing, Expression):	Number of Words: _____ Number of Errors: _____ Self-Corrections: _____	

Accuracy Rate: RW-E/RWx100		Self-Correction Rate: (E+SC) /SC= 1:	

Figure 5.17b: Running Record Comprehension Check

(continues)

Figure 5.17b *(continued)*

Name_____ Date_____ Grade_____

Ask the student to retell the text. Say, "Please tell what happened in the text, including all important parts." Record what the reader says. If the reader is having trouble, ask *general* prompts such as:

What happened first?

Is there anything else? What happened after _____ (say something the child *said*)

Why?

Then, evaluate the retelling according to the categories below.

Questions to Evaluate Retell	

Does the reader have the central meaning of the text? Does she include the most important information?
 	
   No   Partial   Yes
   1 2 3	

Does the reader organize the retelling?
 	
  Not   Somewhat Logical/Sequential
Organized Organized
   1 2 3	

What language patterns or vocabulary is the reader using? Simple Effective/Varied Complex/Precise 1 2 3	
Does the reader exhibit a metacognitive response to the story/ information? Examples include: inference, prediction, connection, opinion/critique No Limited Adequate Extensive 1 2 3 4	

(continues)

Figure 5.17b *(continued)*

Record of Oral Reading	Error	Self Correction	Error	Self Correction
			Meaning Syntax Visual	Meaning Syntax Visual

KEEP IN MIND

When using small-group instruction to meet the needs of struggling learners, it is important not to be overwhelmed by planning, implementing, and record keeping. Keep the following three tips in mind:

1. Start small! There are myriad ways that you can teach struggling learners in small groups. If many seem new to you, or if you have not implemented some of the structures successfully, then start small. Take on one new type of small-group instruction with a few struggling learners in your classroom, and see how that goes.

2. Don't sweat the small stuff! This is just as important in teaching as it is in life. Create a plan of action, and let it unfold. There will be fire drills, snow days, students who are absent, groups that don't seem to gel, teaching points that aren't sticking, and so on. It will happen, and it will be okay. Set a goal you want to accomplish, and don't sweat the small stuff that seems to creep into our days.

3. Reflect and revise! Just like good writers, good teachers reflect and revise. If the strategy lesson didn't work, try again with a different text. If the craft groups seem hard for your struggling learners, add in scaffolds or skip that type of small-group instruction. Be sure to reflect on what is working, celebrate your hard work and accomplishments, and move from there!

CHAPTER SIX

Develop Learning and Study Skills

It is a busy night at Newark Airport. It is, after all, two days before Thanksgiving, and flight volume is high. Air traffic controllers have quite a job to do—they need to manage both takeoffs and arrivals, from multiple runways, for dozens of planes, simultaneously. Even the weather is an element. It is a cloudy night, and the low fog is causing visibility issues. I watch as planes land, but it was getting increasingly difficult to see the planes in flight. I look over at the arrival monitor and notice my flight, along with many others, is delayed. I'm frustrated, but I know that air traffic controllers make difficult but necessary decisions.

Our brain is just like that air traffic control system. It needs to manage focus, control impulses, remember information, make decisions, and reroute as necessary. This is what is known as our executive functioning system, and it is frequently compared to an air traffic control tower for good reason. "Just as we rely on our well-developed personal 'air traffic control system' to make it through our complex days without stumbling, young children depend on their emerging executive function skills to help them as they learn to read and write, remember the steps in performing an arithmetic problem, take part in class discussions or group projects, and enter into and sustain play with other children. The increasingly competent executive functioning of childhood and adolescence enable children to plan and act in a way that makes them good students, classroom citizens, and friends" (Center on the Developing Child 2011).

Executive functions are the brain processes that enable us to initiate, manage, and regulate our time, tasks, and emotions. Our students need good facility with these habits and processes, which include focusing, planning, prioritizing, and managing tasks, as well as managing time, emotions, and distractions flexibly and in relation to context.

As a classroom teacher, I always believed that teaching learning and study skills—the learning to learn or habits of mind skills—is equally if not more important than teaching content. Sure, content is important, but learning study habits and dispositions and developing executive functioning skills are what will make students successful. To ensure that our struggling students are happy and successful in our classrooms, make time to teach learning and study skills.

#26 *Teach the Concept of Time Management Through a Reading Record (1–8)*

Time management is the ability to manage our time in relation to our tasks, expectations, and deadlines. This is not only a school skill but a necessary skill for everyday life.

Most students do not have strong time-management skills. Struggling students have even weaker time-management skills, as they typically underestimate the amount of time a task will take. It is important to provide our students with tools and strategies that will help them manage their time in and out of school.

The best way to begin this work is to build a student's sense of time for how long it takes to complete tasks and assignments. Struggling students frequently have a slower processing speed and take longer to complete tasks. This has no bearing on their ability per se, as many students with a slower processing rate are what is known as "slow and accurate" and have the full capability to handle the cognitive load. Students need support identifying how long a task may actually take.

One area where this skill is especially important is reading. All disciplines require reading, and reading in the content areas, whether math, science, social studies, or a foreign language, can become especially dense and complex. It helps students to know and identify how long it will take to read a text, passage, book, or math problem.

Ask students to track how long it takes to read something. This activity is different from a reading log, which is often used as an accountability tool. In fact, I am proposing the opposite: a short-term timing tool so that students can identify how long it takes to read something and use that knowledge to manage their time.

Begin by asking students to track their reading for two weeks. Provide a timing tool, and ask them to record how long they read and how much they read. For example, if they read in class for 15 minutes, they jot down 15 minutes in the timing tool and then begin reading. Figure 6.1 is an example of a timing tool for reading.

READING RECORD

DATE	TIME READING	TITLE	AUTHOR	AMOUNT READ	REFLECTION ON READING

Sample

DATE	TIME READING	TITLE	AUTHOR	AMOUNT READ	REFLECTION ON READING
5-8-17	20 minutes, school	*Tales of a Fourth Grade Nothing*	Judy Blume	15 pages	Met my 14-page goal.

Figure 6.1: Example of a Timing Tool for Reading

After they read, students in grades 1 and 2 may record book titles, authors, and page numbers. Students in grades 3–8 also record title and author, but may instead record page numbers, number of words, or number of chapters read. After they record how much they read, ask students to reflect on their reading goal. Did they read the amount they set out to read? More than they expected? Less? Does this compare to other days? Did genre, time of day, subject, and so on impact their timing?

Be careful not to qualify their reading as good or bad, or suggest that reading faster is better. Sure, we want to be efficient at all tasks, but if a student has a slower reading or processing speed, the more effective form of support is to first teach time management.

After students have used the timing tool, they can then begin to use other planning tools that will make reading, projects, and studying manageable and successful.

#27   *Provide Tools to Help Schedule and Manage Work and Projects (K–8)*

Provide students with tools that will enable them to schedule and manage work and projects. In *Engaging Every Learner* (Vitale-Reilly, 2015), I suggest a few tools that enable learners to be cognitively engaged in their learning. They provide our struggling students with specific artifacts they can use to manage and schedule their time and their learning. These tools, otherwise known as planners, provide support in two major ways. First, they scaffold time management so that students can learn what time management looks like and feels like. Second, they model how to manage time in direct and explicit ways so that our students learn this seminal skill. Figure 6.2 shows an example of a time management planner.

Here are the steps:

1. Introduce the tool to students. This introduction can be directed at the whole class, small group, or an individual student. Explain what the tool contains: *This planner has multiple parts. It has the days of the week down the left hand side of the page and across the top it lists school and home with space for you to write what you will be working on.*

2. Include any information that is pertinent and nonnegotiable. For example, if students are managing time for a larger project, provide the due date for the final product as well as a midpoint check-in. During the midpoint check-in, review students' idea/hypothesis, their research, and drafts before the final project is due.

MY _____ PLANNER		
Name	Due Date	
DAY	**SCHOOL**	**HOME**
Monday		
Tuesday		
Wednesday		
Thursday		
Friday		

Figure 6.2: Example of a Time-Management Planner

3. Model how to use the planner. Use any of the following teaching options:

- The teacher models and creates a fictitious planner as an example. You might say: *I know that the hypothesis statement is due this Friday, and I am still considering multiple options so I am going to allot two days for this . . .*

- Ask a student from your class to demonstrate how to fill out the planner.

- Fill in the planner with all students collaboratively. Using the collaborative example, students can create individual planners for future projects/tasks.

4. Check in with students during the process about their work, their planner, and their timing. Ask questions such as: *How did that due date go? Did you assign too much work? Did you need to have steps in between? Did the timing feel comfortable? Did you notice a difference between school and home or day to day?* Being reflective about the process will clue them in to what is working and what is not—this is key to learning time-management skills. There is no right or wrong with time management, only an ability to manage time based on your needs, habits, stamina, capacities, and the external requirements or expectations.

#28 *Introduce and Cultivate Focus (K–8)*

It may seem strange to think about cultivating focus. After all, isn't focus one of these things that you either have or don't have? Isn't asking a student to focus like asking her to breathe or sleep? Actually, no. Although natural abilities can vary, focus can be improved, cultivated, and taught.

We want to provide students with strategies for noticing their attention and focus as well as tools for cultivating their ability to stay tuned in to their work. What matters most is that students, with the help of a teacher, create a routine for focus.

In Chapter 1, I explain why it's important to have multiple seating arrangements, and I unpack the idea of a smart spot for learning. In essence, the smart spot is where you can do your best thinking; it's also about working in a place where you can focus. During my time with a kindergarten class this past year, we examined what focus would look like during reading workshop and used the phrase, "getting in a quiet bubble" during independent reading. The teacher and I modeled what being in a quiet bubble would look and sound like, and we taught students how to choose a spot that was conducive to reading. Finding a smart spot and getting in a quiet bubble is the first part of cultivating focus.

Next, you want to be sure to teach students to recognize when their attention is waning so they can employ focus strategies at that moment. In *The Independent Reading Assessment,* Jennifer Serravallo (2012) refers to this as catching your running mind (T8), which is about noticing when your mind is wandering and your focus is waning. Explore focus in one-to-one conversations with students, and try to determine when this happens or even what this feels like. Second grader Luke usually clues into his waning reading focus a few pages after he has lost his attention. He describes it as "coming out of a cloud and realizing that he has no idea what just happened in the book." Through conversations with his teacher, he also realized that when he has a lot of questions about a part, a character, or a chapter, he tends to lose focus. Determine when and where focus exists, when and where focus is lost, and what this looks like for students.

To develop focus or combat waning focus, teach students to do the following:

❑ ***Focus on the right things.*** Struggling learners can be distracted by worries, multiple tasks, or multiple moving parts in our day. In addition, they may be trying to focus on too many things at once—something that ironically leads to a lack of focus. Provide them with ways to remove what they don't need to be focused on to make time and space for what they do need to be focused on. For example, Megan, a fifth grader, becomes very easily distracted by the moving parts of her math workshop. Ellen, her teacher, usually reiterates to Megan that she needs to work on the five practice problems of the day before working on any group project or long-term work. Before she gets started each day, Megan removes any materials that are not related to the practice problems and states to herself her daily goal (as a reminder and focal point). Social elements can also distract students. Ellory, a second-grade student, is always thinking about who she will sit with at lunch, to the point that it distracts her from her class work. When her teacher, Lindsay, finally realized what was distracting Ellory, they made a plan to discuss lunch-time seating during the morning unpacking routine. This seemingly simple move went a long way in keeping Ellory from becoming distracted by the pressure of navigating the social world of lunchtime.

❑ ***Take a break.*** Consistent focus takes time to develop, and taking a break is enormously helpful to struggling students. "I need a break" was one of the nonverbal signals students used in my classroom, and I acknowledged and honored a student's need to stop, break, and regroup. In addition to having a way to signal the need for a break, it is helpful to have a routine for the break. For example, third grader Jack leaves his classroom, walks past the boys' bathroom, loops back to take a quick sip from the water fountain, and returns to his classroom ready to focus. You can teach older students to be more proactive about breaks, chunking out work and preplanning breaks. This can actually help them to build stamina and stretch the amount of time they stay focused. Mark, a sixth grader, determines how long he will work before he takes a break. He plans this either by time or task (work for half the period or read a chapter or part). He has been working toward stretching the amount of time he can focus.

❏ ***Be mindful of and combat distractions.*** Our world is full of distractions, seemingly more each year, and knowing how distractions affect our focus is paramount to success as a student. Teach students to self-advocate about where they will work, noise level in the room, distractions from technology or school PA systems, and basic needs (using the restroom, thirst, hunger). Provide struggling students with the opportunity to attend to their needs. For example, at the beginning of his seventh-period social studies class each day Peter needs a snack, which he eats quickly and quietly, and is then ready to focus. Provide students with tools to tune out distractions. Jerry sits in an area of his classroom where he can quietly hum to himself during independent practice time, and Sammy keeps a squeeze ball in her backpack that she takes out during lessons. She squeezes the ball during any direct instruction or multistep directions. What seem like distractions themselves (small movement and quiet noise) actually help some kids focus.

#29 *Develop Task Initiative (K–8)*

Task initiative is the ability to get started on work in a timely manner. However, many struggling students find this challenging. Challenges with task initiative can be a sign that a student might have a learning disability, and the behavior can manifest itself in different ways.

In the primary grades, I see challenges with task initiative play out in a few common ways: a student takes forever to unpack his belongings, even though you have reviewed the routine numerous times; the learner takes a significant amount of time to get started after the writing minilesson—he sharpens his pencil, asks to get a drink of water, has something he absolutely must tell you. In upper-elementary or middle school we may see a student who also exhibits similar behaviors that are clearly about delaying a task at hand, or we may see that assignments, whether nightly homework or long-term projects, are late or only partially completed.

The issue is not motivation. Typically, these students want to get started and want to do well, but they are lacking the skills to do so. Here are a few steps to support these students:

❏ ***Teach them to have a plan.*** What will you do to get started on your work? For primary students it can be as simple as verbalizing a plan to sharpen pencils in the morning or at the end of the previous day. Or, it might be making a plan to get your writing on your desk before the lesson so you can go to your smart spot and get started right after the lesson. Students in grades 3–8 can make a T-chart of how the day/period will start—What I Will Do/What I Won't Do— and follow through on that behavior. Or, switch up the medium and have students visualize or sketch how they will get started that day, on that project, or every time a certain event occurs in class (such as when a quiz is given or when independent practice begins). Creating a plan verbally, in writing, or via drawing can be quite effective in helping students start tasks promptly.

❏ ***Check in to scaffold their start.*** At the end of a minilesson, I ask students to stay in the meeting area if they are unclear about what to do during independent work time. I want to build a system of trust in classrooms, one where students can be authentic and confident in their ability to communicate struggles. Frequently, struggling learners stay in the meeting area. I assess and then take action. Sometimes students need clarification. For those students I quickly clarify a point or reteach and send them off. Many times, I am left with students who have trouble getting started. I know this is the challenge because they can articulate what was taught but are not ready to work. I have a conversation with these students about the work. I may ask them to envision what their work will look like that day, literally pointing to the page and visualizing where that work will go. I may ask them to state what they will be working on, and I usually ask them to state it as a three-step process: get the materials they need for the lab, make a hypothesis with their partner, and start the experiment. I may even do some brainstorming with them about the topic or the subject of the day before I send them off to work. This quick check-in is a great way for you to scaffold the start.

#30 *Develop Expertise Through Review and Study Guides (3–8)*

Students are more successful when they understand the information they are studying and become "experts" in the concept, process, or information. Sometimes struggling students have a surface level of understanding at the end of a chapter or unit, and they end up spending an enormous amount of unproductive time spinning their wheels. In addition, they try to self-teach when they should be reviewing, and both can be extremely frustrating. We can support them by reviewing material with them to build their expertise, that is, conceptual knowledge and understanding, and provide them with a study guide to scaffold the process.

The idea that it's important to have a deep level of understanding is not new. In a study using chess experts and chess novices, Chase and Simon (1973) concluded that experts were able to chunk information quickly and efficiently and, therefore, were able to remember the position of chess pieces on the board. Success was not determined by how long the players looked at the chessboard or the fact that the information was presented visually. Instead, it was because of the chess players' level of expertise.

To support study skills in struggling learners, we want to begin by making them "experts" in information and concepts.

Here is a recommended process:

1. Review learning with students. One way I have successfully done this is through graffiti conversations. Graffiti conversations are conversations that occur in response to a prompt, question, event, word, or concept. The teacher will ask the question or put forth the prompt or concept and ask for students to respond. The conversation can occur on a bulletin board, chart paper, a tablecloth, a sidewalk with sidewalk chalk, or virtually on a platform such as Padlet. The idea is that students respond to the learning and concept and then respond to each other, thus layering and building their understanding. This activity primes them for effective studying.

2. Once students have reviewed for an assessment, provide them with a study guide. Study guides enable struggling learners to be successful because they remove the obstacle of knowing or deciding what to study. It allows learners to focus their time and energy on studying and reviewing information. Study guides are most effective when they are for a specific amount of information (e.g., a chapter, unit, or concept) and when that information is clear to the learner. Study guides are an important tool for all subjects.

3. Add in time to teach how to use a study guide, and envision it as the scaffold it is intended to be. After you provide the guide, teach students the chunking and planning strategy, instructing them how to divide studying into manageable clusters or chunks. For example, break down the study guide into manageable "chunks," and help students make a three- to five-day study plan, moving through the steps of review, study, and review of the material. Layering the study guide

with the skill of chunking and planning is an example of not just giving the fish (the study guide) but teaching students how to fish (planning and managing studying).

4. Teach students how to read and study a study guide. Show them how to use the self-test study method: *Look, Say, Cover, Look,* outlined in move #31.

   - Look at the word, fact, or idea.

   - State the word/definition, fact, or idea.

   - Cover and again state the word/definition, fact, or idea.

   - Check to see if correct.

As with any strategy, use study guides according to the principles of the Gradual Release of Responsibility (Pearson and Gallagher 1983). Progressively, students can and will own more of the study process and will require less scaffolding as the year goes on.

 ## Explicitly Teach Study Strategies (1–8)

Struggling students often exhibit a disparity between what they know and understand and how they perform on assessments. Although poor test and task performance can be related to a lack of understanding, it is more often related to a challenge with studying.

Studying should be an active process. That means that you are minds on and the time you put in matches the outcome you experience. We can teach struggling students explicit study strategies to be successful during on-demand tasks and tests.

Successful students have techniques for studying that work well for them. My favorite is the *Look, Cover, Say, Look* strategy. This method can be used for students of all ages in a variety of disciplines from math (math facts or remembering algorithms), spelling (learning and studying spelling patterns, families, and words), science (concepts, vocabulary), social studies (dates, names, and events of historical significance), and English language arts or foreign language (vocabulary and rules of syntax). When using this strategy, students look/read the fact, date, or word in an active way. They can use an index card to block out other information, read the information aloud to themselves or to a peer, or highlight or trace the information when they look at it. This practice will help them to not only read but also to process the information. Next, they cover the information and say it to themselves. They can subvocalize (state silently in their head), say it aloud, and even repeat it a few times. Finally, students look again at the information to check whether their "say" was correct.

Here are a few other study strategies that work well with struggling students:

- Make flash cards with index cards or on a technology tool such as Quizlet or Kahoot! Be sure to determine which method—print or digital—works best for the student. Some struggling students benefit from the newer technology programs that incorporate digital flash cards, and some do much better with print options. The tangibility of the actual index card adds a tactile layer that will benefit some learners.

- After they have study tools, students can ask someone to quiz them, or students can self-quiz.

- Explain what they are studying to someone else—explain it as facts, or make it a story.

- Read notes or study guides out loud, pointing to the words as you go.

#32 *Develop Note-Taking Skills (3–8)*

The ability to take notes on concepts, ideas, and new learning is one of the most essential skills our students need for future academic success. We expect students to take notes, and we want them to use their notes frequently, yet we seldom spend enough time teaching our students *how* to take notes.

Many people advocate for the use of organizers and teacher-created tools to scaffold note-taking work. I actually believe these aren't the best choice, even for our struggling students. Organizers ask students to fit their thinking into sections, boxes, and parts determined by someone else. The organization of the tool may or may not make sense to the student, and struggling learners frequently spend their time and energy trying to figure out what they should write, where. Trying to take notes while listening to a teacher can be catastrophic. Some students are unable to listen and note relevant information in the boxes. Taking notes while reading can be equally unproductive. The way students receive and process the information may not match the tool you created, and again, students expend energy trying to determine what they are "supposed to put in the boxes" on the note-taking page. There are three other options:

Option 1: Individualize note-taking tools. Our learners are all so different that one tool is not effective. For example, Rishun is quite artistic. She has the ability to represent learning and understanding beautifully and accurately through pictures. In addition, she is not bothered by a lot of information on a page. This is different from David. David cannot record or process when too much information is on the page. Therefore, he needs to create space between the notes on the page. In addition, he benefits from having lines in his note-taking tools. This situation is also different from Jordan's, who is linear in his thinking. His note-taking goes best when he takes a series of notes in short phrases right down the page, list-like. Could one note-taking form or format work for all these different learners? I do not believe so. It is best to teach students to take notes by allowing them to "muck about." Read a short passage or watch a quick video clip, and model how you would put information on a page. Vocalize the metacognitive aspect of your process, and demonstrate how you approach the task. You might say: *I like to start my notes with a title. This reminds me what the big idea, question, or source is. So, let me record that here in the box that I made on the top of the page. I know that when I watch videos, the information is going to be divided into parts, and sometimes the video has words that are important to know and understand. So, each time I learn about a new part, I put a line and write the big idea. I try to only write a few words down. Then, after listening (or reading, if this were in a text), I record what I think is most important to write down. I do this with bullets, but if an image pops into my head, or if the video provides a diagram or visual, I might make a quick sketch.* You might also show students notes from other students. Rishun and Jordan's notes are a far better example than mine! After you model, give students time to practice taking notes, trying different formats and and techniques across disciplines. Talk about what is working and what is not working. This really solidifies their note-taking process. Figure 6.3 is a sample of student designed note-taking.

Option 2: Offer open-ended organizers. If you feel that it would be better to provide students with an organizer, then I recommend that you offer open-ended ones, and then model how students might use those different organizers. Struggling students benefit from utilizing tools that allow them to provide answers and thinking in concise and accessible ways. For example, rather than creating a paragraph to describe a character's change across a text, students can use a graphic organizer to depict their understanding. One such organizer could be a flow map (www.thinkingmaps.com). This would allow students to sequence and identify the change across time to demonstrate their comprehension. This tool removes the obstacle of composition and flow of thoughts while it simultaneously allows the teacher to gauge comprehension and depth of thinking.

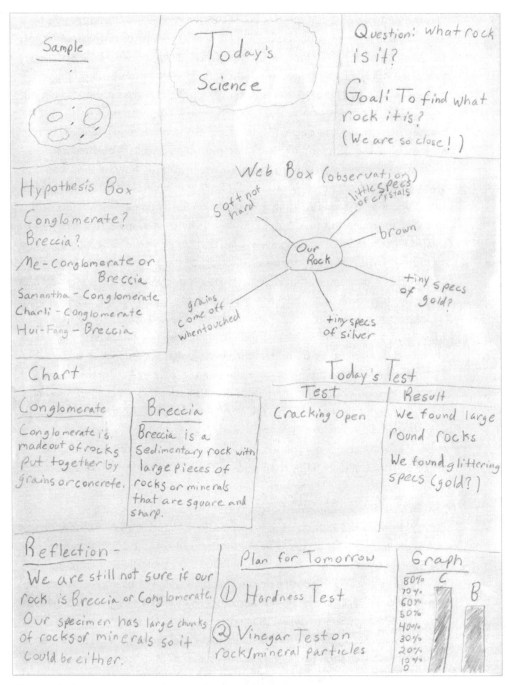

Figure 6.3: Sample of Student Designed Note-taking

Again, start by modeling how to use the various note-taking formats, allow them to try taking notes in a variety of contexts (across disciplines if this is available, or even just in different situations: after reading, during lessons, while watching a podcast), and then reflect on what is working or not working.

I highly recommend the Cornell note-taking method. In the Cornell method, students divide their page into three categories: a somewhat large margin on the left for questions and key points, the remainder of the page to take notes, and a box at the bottom to summarize and reflect on learning. It is structured enough to support the learner, yet open enough for them to manage before, during, and after note-taking. Figure 6.4 is an example of the Cornell method. Some of my favorite open-ended organizers are from Thinking Maps (www .thinkingmaps.com) because they are versatile and can be used by a variety of different learners.

Option 3: Teach Text Coding. Text coding is a strategy a reader can use to code a text with a symbol that represents their thinking. The symbol can represent a question, new learning, a contradiction, or even a surprising part. The coding I use is similar to what Harvey Daniels and Nancy Steineke (2011) present in *Texts and Lessons for Content Area Reading*. See figure 6.5 for codes that can be used to note and annotate texts during reading.

TITLE:	
Key Points: *Students jot the key points, questions, or sections.*	**Notes:** *Students take notes on the key points or sections in this portion.* *Note-taking works best when the notes:* • *Are not written in full sentences* • *Are organized as lists* • *Contain any symbol or quick sketch to illustrate points* • *Are spaced for easier access later*
Summary: *Students can provide a few sentences about the main ideas from today's notes. This section can be completed right after notes are taken or as a follow-up (for home study or the next day).*	

Figure 6.4: Cornell Note-Taking Method

CODE	WHAT IT MEANS
+	Something new I have learned
✱	Something important, key, powerful
!	Something surprising, wonderful
✔	Something I already knew
X	Something that contradicts my knowledge
?	Something I have a question about; need clarification
O	Words or phrases that are unknown

Figure 6.5: Text Coding Symbols

KEEP IN MIND

Many of the "study and learning" skills addressed in this chapter are executive functions that serve us well in both career and life. Therefore, when implementing these moves, I recommend the following:

- Remember that all learners are different. Therefore, try the variety of tools and resources suggested, but also don't be afraid to allow students to modify or create their own. For example, Rishun came up with her own note-taking page, and not only was it far superior to the ones that I suggested, it fit her perfectly. I think the motto, "adopt, adapt, create" works well with finding the study tools and processes that work for each individual.

- Don't forget to build in time to try. The only way we know if a tool, resource, or process works is if we try it. The more low-stakes the try-it is (for example, trying for a weekly assignment, rather than for a big unit project), the better the learner fares.

- Don't forget to build in time to reflect. Reflection is key to process and habit building, so be sure to ask learners how the tool, resource, or process worked and whether or not they think it will help them.

CHAPTER SEVEN

*T*each Communication Skills

Now, more than ever, our students need effective communication skills to be successful, happy, and productive citizens of our classrooms and our world. Next-generation standards support this. ELA standards, whether the CCSS or a state-designed version, all call for the development of speaking and listening skills including asking and answering questions; describing people, places, and events; participating in collaborative conversations; instituting moves such as piggybacking, agreeing or disagreeing, and gaining the floor in respectful ways; and presenting ideas to a variety of audiences and for a variety of purposes (CCSS 2010). Our next-generation science standards, the NGSS, also look toward speaking and listening skills as they too require students to take recently learned content and generate a solution to a problem, offer an opinion on various scientific issues, participate in collaborative conversations, and present ideas.

Effective communication presents a challenge for many struggling learners. Some learners might have difficulty with language and may even have a language disability. Some might have a learning difference, weakness, or learning disability that is affected by underdeveloped listening and processing skills. And for others, their struggles with presentation and communication are a direct result of articulation and/or spoken language fluency issues.

The good news is that communication skills can be taught and developed, even with our struggling learners.

#33 Develop Conversation Skills Through Whole-Class Conversations (2–8)

There are some folks who seem to have innate conversation skills. They have the "gift for gab" as my Nanny used to say, and it seems as if conversation is fun and effortless for them. But it does not mean that we can't develop conversation skills if they don't come naturally. These skills can be learned by all students, including and especially those who struggle.

My favorite way to do this is to provide lots of time to have guided conversations. Although I am typically a fan of differentiating through small-group instruction and one-on-one conferences, guided practice through whole-class conversations is effective.

Whole-class conversations can happen around a text (novel, short story, video, image, content area chapter, article, or blog) or a concept. One way to develop conversation skills, and simultaneously prepare students for reading and writing partnerships and clubs, is to have whole-class conversations about the instructional read-aloud. The idea is that the large group is going to come around one idea and talk together. In this model, the teacher serves as the facilitator or "guide on side" but allows students to do most of the talking.

Whole-class conversations are based in Lev Vygotsky's theory of More Knowledgeable Other (1978), the theory that when students interact under the guidance of a more knowledgeable person, or a learner who has more experience or further developed skills, we all develop our skills in that area.

Here, the more knowledgeable others are both the teacher and certain students—the ones with the gift for gab—and the structure of whole-class conversations provides the forum. Here is how a whole-class conversation can go:

- The class comes around a concept, idea, or text.

- The concept, idea, or text is put forth, and a specific topic of conversation is agreed upon. In the early stages of whole-class conversation, the teacher may put forth the specific topic of conversation. However, as the structure continues to be utilized, students put forth possibilities and then agree upon the specific topic.

COMMON SCAFFOLDS	HOW THIS MIGHT GO
Use a prop to guide the conversation.	Think of a speaking stick or the conch from *Lord of the Flies*. An object or prop is used to guide the conversation in order to maintain a pace that is conducive for those who process or articulate more slowly, or in order to allow quieter, less overt voices to enter the conversation. A student demonstrates his or her desire to speak (a thumbs up or nod, for example). The person who just spoke passes the object to that person as the next speaker. This prop can also scaffold connecting ideas in a conversation if the object is passed to someone who can piggyback, agree, or thoughtfully and, in a connected way, turn a corner.
Students can help other students enter the conversation.	Sometimes, students want to speak, but they are reluctant to insert themselves into a conversation. When this is the case, another scaffold that works well is to have a buddy who can help. Tommy and Jason were good friends, and together they figured out that Tommy's lack of participation was not because Tommy had nothing to say; it was because of Tommy's language and processing differences. So, Tommy and Jason would sit next to each other, and when Tommy wanted to speak, he tapped Jason. Jason, in his expert, extroverted way would say, "Tommy would like to speak," and Tommy did. This scaffold helped Tommy learn to process his thinking and join the conversation more naturally. He was no longer stressed about how he would enter the conversation (Jason would do this part for him) so he could focus on processing ideas and formulating what he wanted to say.
Move slowly and thoughtfully through conversations by repeating key ideas.	Again, this scaffold is instituted by an MKO—first the teacher, and then students. Every so often an MKO would say one of the following: So what we have been discussing. . . . What I hear people saying is. . . . John just put forth the idea that. . . . This scaffold accommodates those who may have trouble following the conversation, whether it is due to the amount that needs to be processed or the pace of the conversation. Either way, this scaffold keeps the talk going and connected. See Move #10 for more information on using scripted conversation starters to scaffold conversations.

- An MKO (more knowledgeable other) starts the conversation. Again, this can be the teacher, who can gradually release the floor to students who wish to start the conversation.

- Others join in the conversation. No hands are raised. Why no hands? When have you ever raised your hand in a conversation with another person? Never. Therefore, no hands here. The typical rule of thumb is that if two people go to speak at once, one defers to the other, and that person who deferred will speak next.

- The teacher monitors and observes. She may jump in to pause on an essential point so the community can say more, invite others into the conversation, connect ideas stated, reiterate an idea, or turn the corner.

- Gradually, all are asked to speak. Scaffolds are put into place to support quieter voices, less confident speakers, students with language impairments, or slow processers. Conversely, those who tend to speak a lot may be asked to make room for other voices.

- Develop conversation stamina. At first, whole-class conversations may be three minutes long, but with practice, they can be ten to fifteen minutes.

- Reflect to improve conversation. After the conversation, the group reflects. What went well? Where were the trouble spots? Who had trouble getting into the conversation? What can we do about that? In the beginning, the reflection takes as much time as the conversation so that the skills are internalized and issues can move forward to a more positive place.

Whole-class conversations provide struggling learners with plenty of models and time to practice conversation skills. Students can then take the newly acquired skills into small-group and partner conversations.

 #34 *Support Auditory Understanding (K–8)*

Another communication issue that plagues struggling students is processing the amount of talk that happens in a school day. Students with learning disabilities or learning differences may suffer from weak auditory understanding. The student may exhibit the following behaviors: She appears unfocused; she looks as if she is not listening; she asks for something to be repeated often, sometimes accompanied by a what? or huh?; she has difficulty following directions; or even some combination of the above behaviors. Listening to and understanding what others say is such an important part of communication, both in school and in everyday life, so implement moves that support auditory understanding.

One way to do this is to restate, paraphrase, or rephrase.

> **Restate:** Students who have communication issues that impact processing need time to process what was just said. I describe this as their ears "heard" you, but their brain did not. In this instance, it doesn't actually help the student if you say something different, even if you think you are simplifying or clarifying information. What happens here is they now need to reprocess, starting over, trying to learn what you just said. Therefore, it is best if you repeat the information, using the exact phrasing and word order. By repeating the information, the learner who needs processing time has a second chance to process the original sentence and thus create understanding. Conversations and communications can then proceed.

> **Paraphrase:** For some struggling students, auditory understanding is impacted by the complexity or speed of the communication. Therefore, these students benefit from paraphrasing. Whether it's a statement or concept, state it differently, slowly, and more concretely. Paraphrasing ideas and modifying the speed of the exchange allows the student to focus on certain key words and ideas without the distraction of complex ideas or vocabulary. When I use this technique, I tend to use both the original complex thought and the modified, paraphrased idea. It might go something like this: *In the water cycle, the second stage is condensation. During condensation, the water condenses: it shrinks and comes together and then turns back into water.* Notice that I did not eliminate the word *condensation* but paraphrased and modified it to include simpler, more concrete and familiar terminology. Paraphrasing supports auditory understanding because it allows the conversation to occur at more comprehensible pace.

> **Rephrase:** Rephrasing or restating a sentence or idea helps support auditory understanding. Begin this move by modeling. You might rephrase using phrases like, *So again...* Or, *What I heard you say is. . . .* Eventually, I turn the rephrasing over to the student. For example, during a guided reading lesson using the chapter titled "Catalog Cats" in *The Stories Julian Tells*, I used rephrasing with one third-grade student, Jessica. I asked the group, "What is it you are looking for in today's reading of 'Catalog Cats'? Jessica, can you say back to me what it is you are looking for?" All students were held accountable by the question, but for Jessica, being asked to define the task and state the learning from the lesson enabled her to process the task and articulate it to me and to the group. This move provided Jessica with a direct prompt and gave her time to process and answer.

#35   *Teach Students to Self-Advocate (K–8)*

Teaching students to self-advocate puts them front and center in their own learning. How many times have you thought, "I'm not exactly sure if they understood," or "They look like they are listening, but they are not able to answer or articulate new ideas," or "I know they didn't understand, but I am not sure what they need." When this is the case, teaching students to self-advocate is the answer.

- Create a community where it is okay to be unsure. Let students know that all of us need clarification at some point. There are moments when we all misunderstand, don't hear clearly, or are unsure. It happens to all of us, not just struggling learners.

- Teach students to identify the moment when a misunderstanding occurs. This is an important step. Some students might be able to notice right away if they are unclear, but struggling students need time to "know when they don't know." I usually model this by demonstrating what it looks and feels like to be confused in a conversation. For example, suddenly all of the words sound like Charlie Brown's teacher (blah, blah, blah, as if you are under water). Or, I find that my mind has wandered, and I no longer understand what has been said. Or, my mind feels like it is on delay. Something was said, but I need a minute to catch up to what that was. Recognize it, acknowledge it, and then know what to do about it.

- Provide them with specific phrases and sentences to use when they are unclear:
  - ➤ I do not understand. Can you say that again?
  - ➤ Please repeat that. I am not sure what you said.
  - ➤ Can you pause? I need a minute to catch up.
  - ➤ What do you mean when you say…?
  - ➤ I heard the part where you said . . . but do not know what you said after that.
  - ➤ Can you explain that?

These phrases allow students to advocate for their needs and provide them with an increasing amount of responsibility and agency over what they understand and what they need repeated, restated, or explained.

- Acknowledge and celebrate their self-advocacy. When students receive positive reinforcement for their self-advocacy efforts, they will take action more frequently, positively, and with great success.

#36 *Cultivate Presentation Skills (2–8)*

Frequently, both in life and school, we are asked to present our ideas, information, take on a topic or situation, or thinking. As one aspect of communication, making a presentation is not only an essential academic and life skill, it is one that many people struggle with. There are a myriad of reasons why students may struggle—challenges with articulation and expression, organization issues, and nervousness when presenting or speaking in public. Here are three sure-fire ways to cultivate the presentation skills of struggling learners:

1. Provide presentation formats. Formats simplify communication and provide our struggling learners with a simple and engaging format. Try the format used for Ignite Talks. Ignite Talks are five minutes in length, accompanied by twenty slides, with fifteen seconds to present each slide. Ignite Talks started in Seattle in 2006 and have spread to many different organizations and venues. If you have ever attended an Edcamp, you saw that Ignite Talks are the driving structure. With struggling students, I adapt the Ignite Talk format slightly to accommodate their strengths and needs, as well as project parameters. Meet with each student to decide together on an amount of time that makes sense. Consider the number of slides and the amount of content on each slide. Don't limit the length of time for each slide; instead, adjust the time to meet the needs of each student. You'll also want to consider the communication skills of the presenter. A shorter presentation might feel more manageable for some students.

2. Find a presentation mentor, and study presentation techniques and styles. A presentation mentor can serve as an example for struggling learners. Students can use TED Talks and TED-Ed to find great examples of smooth and engaging presentations. I ask students to look for presentation mentors they feel they can emulate. In particular, when viewing and studying mentors, students should look for the following:

Three of my favorite TED Talk mentors are: Arthur Benjamin, "A Performance of 'Mathemagic'" (I love the way he uses the stage and actively engages the audience); Tavi Gevinson, "A Teen Just Trying to Figure It Out "(I love the way she uses humor and unpacks a topic that resonates with the audience); and Susan Cain, "The Power of Introverts" (I love the way she uses anecdotes and how she paces her talk so that the audience really thinks about each idea). All three are great mentors for our students, and their techniques are ones our struggling students can really study and emulate.

QUALITIES OF PRESENTATION STYLES AND TECHNIQUES

PRESENTATION QUALITY	QUESTIONS STUDENTS CAN ASK
Movement	Does the presenter move around, sit, or stand still? How much space does the presenter use? What kind of movement does the presenter make—walking around, hand or facial expressions?
Structure	How does the presentation start? How does the presentation end? When and where do they use visuals or audio?
Content	How does the presenter give information—relevant dates, statistics, data, research? Does the presenter tell stories or share anecdotes? Does the presenter share realizations or reflections?
Style	Is humor used? Do you hear the presenter say things like, "Umm" or "Ah" or other pause noises? How does that affect you as a listener?
Pace	How quickly does the presenter speak? Does the presenter pause? If so, why? Does the information come at you slowly, fast, a combination?

Figure 7.1: Qualities of Presentation Styles and Techniques

3. Use technology such as VoiceThread to practice presenting. We can use technology to enhance the practice experience. My favorite practice technology tool is VoiceThread, which is a web-based application that lets you upload media, add voice, and share with the world. VoiceThread conversations are known as asynchronous conversations. This means that the original creator will upload her docs, add her voice, and then invite others to join in on the conversation. The conversations do not happen at once. Any participant can go on and "join" the conversation at any time. Here, I envision VoiceThread as a tool that can be used to practice presentations and get feedback. First, students upload their presentation, including the media, such as slides, images, videos, or documents, and then they add their oral presentation to the VoiceThread. When they share the uploaded material, peers can to listen to the presentation and give feedback. Offer some guiding questions for student feedback:

- Was the information presented in a clear manner?

- How was the speed of the presentation? Were you able to follow along?

- Was the presentation engaging/interesting? If not, what might make the presentation more interesting? A vignette? An example?

Once students have recorded the VoiceThread for practice, they can listen to the feedback of their peers and revise their presentation based on the feedback. Final versions of the presentation can be delivered live or in a newly recorded VoiceThread.

 # Teach Nonverbal Communication (K–8)

Nonverbal communication is one way we show what we're thinking. Struggling students might have issues reading, interpreting, or using nonverbal communication. We can teach students how to read and use body language, expressions, gestures, and signals.

TEACH STUDENTS TO READ NONVERBAL COMMUNICATION

Use games and scenarios that are both fun and real-world. For example, I play charades with students, where we act out possible social situations—a peer is upset because he feels left out, a teacher needs help quieting the class down, another student wants to talk to you but doesn't know how to begin the conversation, a new student is in your class and doesn't know where to sit. Here is how the game might go:

- As a whole class, and eventually in small groups, provide students with a social scenario (see earlier examples) either verbally or on index cards. Ask for volunteers to act out the scenario without words.

- Ask students who watch the scenario to describe the situation or jot down what they notice on the index card. What is happening? Here, the goal is to have students "see" the situation by reading the nonverbal communication.

- Brainstorm ways to appropriately respond to the situation; make a list on chart paper. Ask volunteers to act out ways to respond to the situation.

I also do a take on Charades where one person is acting out a scenario, and the other person is reacting to it. Students "read" both the action and the reaction and discuss the ways nonverbal communication was used. We explore questions such as: How do we know someone is upset? What does their body look like? What does their face look like? Is there any other movement or motion that is used? Students learn how feelings and thoughts are communicated nonverbally and learn how to better read the nonverbal communication we encounter each day.

Finally, you can create anchor charts with students about what good nonverbal communication can look like. For example, an anchor chart can include:

I Show I Am Listening When I:

✓ Follow the speaker with my eyes

✓ Lean in

✓ Show agreement by nodding or giving a thumbs up

✓ React with a smile

Figure 7.2: Nonverbal Communication Anchor Chart

TEACH STUDENTS TO USE NONVERBAL COMMUNICATION

Teach students nonverbal communication signals as a way to express their needs/wants, emotions, and understanding.

Represent Needs and Wants

Students can use nonverbal signals to communicate anything that fits within the structures and routines of the classroom. One signal that should be a part of every classroom is the one for "I need a break." This signal can be communicated with a hand gesture (I like two fingers, as in "I need two minutes") or via eye contact and a nod. Take the case of Milo, a behavior disabled fifth-grade student who is being mainstreamed into a general education classroom. Both the teacher and the instructional aide need to provide Milo with breaks a few times a day. Based on Milo's classification, breaks help him manage frustration. The key is to provide breaks after Milo has been appropriately encouraged to finish a task or lesson but before his level of frustration reaches peak level. In sports, this is frequently referred to an athlete's "push level." It is essential to determine a struggling student's "push level" and move him to this level but not beyond it. Provide a break so students can regroup and move forward.

Represent Emotions

Students with learning differences and disabilities need productive ways to manage frustration and communicate how they are feeling. Teach students how to use nonverbal signals:

EMOTION	NONVERBAL SIGNAL
Okay	Thumb and pointer together in a circle like an O.
Excited	Thumbs up
Angry	Closed fist
Sad	Two peace fingers pointed down
Happy	Two peace fingers up
Anxious	Thumb and pinky up, shaking

Figure 7.3: Nonverbal Signals for Emotions

Providing struggling students with the ability to communicate their emotions nonverbally will go a long way. Signals can be used exclusively or coupled with a verbal word, phrase, or sentence to not only provide a direct avenue to communication but also scaffold the development of verbal communication.

Represent Understanding

Communicating understanding nonverbally is a great way to get struggling students to demonstrate understanding in an accessible and tangible way. I use the following nonverbal signals to demonstrate understanding:

- Fist to Five. Fist represents no understanding, five fingers represents total understanding, three fingers somewhere in between.
- Circle, Triangle, Square. By marking their page or white board with these symbols, students can communicate total understanding (circle), confusion (square), and a question (triangle).

When we provide students the opportunity to read and use nonverbal signals, we support their communication development.

KEEP IN MIND

Although communication skills are essential everyday life and academic skills, communication is something that most struggling learners grapple with. In fact, communication is something that even neurotypical (students without neurological differences) students need support and scaffolding for. Students who are neurodiverse (students with neurological differences such as ADHD and autism spectrum disorders) not only require moves that support them as they acquire communication skills but need teachers who understand that some communication challenges require an understanding of learning differences and the neurological spectrum.

- Be aware of communication challenges. Typical verbal and nonverbal behaviors can be hard for some struggling students.

- Be respectful of communication differences. Some students have different beliefs around both verbal and nonverbal communication. For example, looking someone in the eye or lengthy social chatting may be difficult or atypical for some learners.

- Be mindful of communication contexts. Some struggling learners feel more comfortable talking to adults, some to peers. Learn the communication preferences of your struggling learners, and note the differences in different contexts. Understanding this can provide you with the key to implementing moves that will support learners most.

CHAPTER EIGHT

Writing Instructional Moves That Help Students Across the Day

It is late March, and my students are hard at work composing their latest writing piece—an informational article based on what they learned in our recent geology unit. A working hum fills the room, and I am excited to see their next drafts. The students are making progress, and I am looking forward to seeing where their writing goes during this last leg of the school year. I look at Emma. She is writing; she is certainly trying, and I could argue that she too is making progress this year. All of this is true. What is also true is that Emma is struggling. I can see it in her face; I can feel it from across the room.

Emma came to my class as a struggling writer. She claimed to hate writing and was reluctant during all the community-building writing exercises we did at the beginning of the year. She found it hard to brainstorm ideas and share her writing. She had difficulty talking about what makes her a good writer. She produced a great narrative piece, but that was tough work, and it seems that Emma is always taking two steps forward and one step back when it comes to writing. Emma demonstrates progress and implements strategies taught in units and conferences, only to forget them the following week. I decide that my conferring will start here, with Emma, and that what she needs is a teaching move that will support her specific struggles: motivation, organization, and development.

Writing is an interesting academic discipline because it travels with our students across the day. It is part of the subject known as language arts (or English), it is its own discrete discipline (different from reading and language use), and it is used across the day (in school and at home). Writing is also part of the communication arts and is used in our daily lives, in big ways and small, from sending a text message, to leaving a "honey do" note on the fridge, to composing wedding vows or a eulogy.

Writing is one of the most important disciplines to teach and practice because it contributes to both academic and life success.

Writing requires a learner to exercise an enormous number of skills. Writing is about fine motor skills—physically getting words on the page. Writing is about idea generation and using thoughts, experiences, research, and knowledge to create text. Writing is also about memory and using schema to fuel writing. Writing requires an understanding of structure and organization, craft, conventions, and rules of language, and most importantly, writing is about synthesis, combining all of the above seamlessly and simultaneously. This is quite a tall order. Learners who have fine and visual motor issues struggle with writing; learners who have short-term or working memory issues may struggle with writing; and students who struggle with attention and focus also may struggle with writing, from idea generation, to writing stamina, to organization and fluency of ideas.

When we consider how we might support struggling learners, we want to use instructional moves that offer support across the day. "One way to ease the processing demands associated with incorporating new procedures into a heavily taxed cognitive system is to explicitly demonstrate how to apply these new tools and then scaffold instruction so that children move from using them with the help of a skilled other (e.g., the teacher) to applying them efficiently and effectively on their own" (Graham and Harris 2005). The instructional moves that have the most positive impact are moves that are direct, explicit, and differentiated to scaffold student learning.

#38 *Model in a Variety of Ways (K–8)*

In my twenty-seven years of teaching, I have learned that the one thing consistent about struggling learners is that they can be inconsistent. I try to remember that what worked one day might not work another day. To combat this, and support struggling writers across the day, I carefully consider *how* I model during lessons. I consider what is challenging for my struggling writers, but more importantly, I consider their strengths and the ways in which they learn best. Then I match what I model to their strengths. There are four ways to model writing in minilessons, conferences, and small-group lessons.

1. Teacher modeling. The key to successful teacher modeling is to remember to write in front of your students, keep it succinct, and model precisely what you are asking them to do. Although it may be appealing to have the work prewritten, I strongly encourage you to write in front of your students. Not only are

they seeing the writing model you create, but they are seeing you model the process of writing—how you start, if you pause, when you slow down or cross out, what comes easily, what challenges you . . . all the ways that you are a writer just like them!

2. Published mentor texts. When looking for mentor texts for struggling learners, remember that the writing needs to match the task in three ways: kind (genre), length, and form (format or structure). In addition, always remember to match students' zone of proximal development (Vygotsky 1978) by choosing texts that will be accessible to them. Structure the lesson as a model – thinking aloud and showing what the text contains, or as an inquiry – where you will do some modeling but will also invite students to notice and name genre elements and craft techniques.

3. Student mentor texts. Sometimes, the best writing mentor is a peer. Be on the lookout for student mentor writing, and save writing from year to year in minilessons and conferences. Store examples of student mentor writing in the classroom, and make sure they're accessible to students during writing time (anchor charts, mentor boards, Google classroom). For more information about using student writing in lessons and conferences, I strongly suggest reading *Learning from Classmates: Using Students' Writing as Mentor Texts* (Eickholdt 2015).

4. Shared writing/language experience. One of the most engaging and supportive ways to model for students is to write *with* them. In a shared writing experience, students cocreate writing with you. In this type of model, the demonstration is highly interactive and minds are on. Each learner contributes to the composition of the piece (by turning and talking, jotting what they would write next, and agreeing to what should go in the shared text), and the teacher and students can both take the lead. Shared writing can even serve as mentor/ model that students use as a springboard for their own writing, with students lifting a part of the shared writing as the first part of their own writing.

#39 *Add Kinesthetic and Tactile Support for Writing (K–8)*

I am a firm believer in the power of kinesthetic movement and tactile support for learning, especially for struggling learners. Why? For them, understanding and remembering multiple parts to a story, multiple steps to a process, and multiple steps necessary to complete a task (whether in a text to be read or written, a historical event, math problem, or a series of directions) can be challenging because of weak working memory. Working memory is a part of the short-term memory system that takes in visual and auditory input and processes and stores the input in the short term, until it can be moved to long-term memory. Information does not go into long-term memory until it is processed in our working memory.

Research on ways to help students with weak working memory supports the notion that it is best to use strategies that decrease working memory stress and overload, rather than try to improve working memory. How can we decrease working memory overload without decreasing the expectations we have for students? We can chunk information and provide students with tangible ways to process this information in the short term. One way to do that is to add kinesthetic movement to the processing procedure. For example, allow students to add physical movement when they are interacting with texts. Here are four ways to add movement to writing:

1. Add movement to retellings. Allow students to move step by step to recall action and events before writing.

2. Role-play or act out memories, experiences, or situations. This can include acting out a sequence of events, a problem or solution a character had, or even a reaction or motivation to the problem.

3. Allow students to plan writing by touching the page. Students will touch each page (or parts of the page) while planning their writing, literally adding the tapping movement while stating the parts of the text. Add an auditory prompt if necessary, such as, what will go here? What will go next?

4. Use objects to generate writing. The object can serve as a reminder of a memory, can be observed to create sensory images, or can be the impetus for opinion writing.

 ## #40 *Get Writing Started by Offering Choices (K–8)*

Motivation is a huge part of writing. Anyone who has ever written anything, ever, knows that. When a task or activity is hard for us, our motivation decreases; our enjoyment, engagement, and success decrease as well.

Research supports this. When students are motivated, they increase their behavioral, cognitive, and emotional engagement and, thus, increase the personal investment they make in learning (Reeve 2016). In addition, motivation can lead learners to bring the habits of mind necessary for success to the task of writing

WAYS TO GIVE WRITERS CHOICES

Tools:
- Instruments—pencils, pens or crayons (for younger students)
- Medium—different kinds of paper, notebooks, computer, handheld device
- Mentor texts—other students' writing, picture books, articles, trade books, newspapers.

Interactions:
- Seating options—where they sit (and on what kind of surface—floor or chair) during lessons and independent practice
- Peer options—working independently or with a partner
- Space options—what parts of the environment they will use while writing.

Writing Topics:
- Topic choice in writing workshop.

  What memory will you choose for your small moment narrative?
- Topic choice in content areas.

  What element of _____ (weather, our animal study, the civil war) will you choose for your _____ (nonfiction chapter book, article, Prezzi)?
- Specific content choice in content writing.

  Choose a cause of air pollution, and demonstrate the effects of this type of pollution in your essay.

Either way, writers need total choice (what I am writing about), or modified self-selection (what I choose related to our whole class study or what I specifically say about a topic given to me) when writing.

Structure, Form, and Genre:
- **Structure:** What will the writing look like on the page? (columns vs. paragraphs, organization of paragraphs or parts, placement of graphics)
- **Form:** Will this piece be a picture book, chapter book, article, essay, google slides, brochure, or itinerary?
- **Genre:** What genre will best express my idea? Narrative, poem, editorial? Providing students choice in genre a few times during the year is essential.

When we provide our writers with choices in structure, form, and genre, we enable them to use their preferences and strengths as writers.

Audience:
Identifying an authentic audience is a great way to motivate writers. An authentic audience is anyone who wants or needs the information. An authentic audience might be:
- The student writer
- Classmates and/or teacher
- The larger school community (other classes, parents and families, principal or literacy coach)
- Online community
- When we allow students to consider and choose the audience, we motivate our writers to persist through the hard work of writing!

Figure 8.1: Ways to Give Writers Choices

including persistence, stamina, time on task, and overall performance. Writers who are motivated will take more risks, spend more time writing, will produce more writing, and will enjoy the task more—all behaviors that will lead to better writing.

Choice is one of the simplest yet most profound ways to motivate a learner. Having choice will motivate students by building enduring rather than situational interest (Cambria and Guthrie 2010). I tend to see a lot of sameness in writing (everyone writes on the same topic, or in the same genre, or in the same form), especially with struggling learners. For some reason, it is believed that telling writers exactly what to do, or specifically what to write about, is easier for them. The opposite is actually true. Asking struggling writers to write in a particular genre or form can be okay some of the time, but remember that students should always have some say in what they do as writers. This will allow them to show their strengths and use what is working for them to push their writing. Figure 8.1 demonstrates the many ways to give writers choice.

#41 *Support Generating Ideas (K–8)*

Although I believe that writers should be able to choose their topic, I do recognize that this can be a challenge for struggling writers. Therefore, I suggest you teach students to find ideas around the big three: people, places, and objects. The big three are universal enough to apply to every writer, yet specific enough to represent a tangible writing idea. To support this work, I:

- Use children's literature as examples of writing about the big three. Figure 8.2 is a list of my favorite anchor texts to use with struggling and reluctant writers. These texts model where writers get ideas and how writers write about people, places, and objects.

- Model your own ideas that are inspired by people, places, and objects. When struggling writers see you model where to get writing ideas, they can see the connection between the writer and the writing. Figure 8.3 is an anchor chart that demonstrates where I get my ideas.

- Provide students with idea-generating tools. Struggling learners benefit from scaffolding tools, and this is certainly true for supporting idea generation. Therefore, I offer students paper that supports their idea generation. For narrative and poetry writing, I title the paper, "My Writing Ideas." For informational writing, "My Expert Ideas," and for opinion or argument writing, "I Care a Lot About. . . ." See Figure 8.4 for an example of a writing paper that supports generating ideas.

ANCHOR TEXTS THAT CAN SUPPORT STRUGGLING LEARNERS TO GENERATE WRITING IDEAS

TITLE	AUTHOR	WHAT THE TEXT DEMONSTRATES
In the Land of Words	Eloise Greenfield	**People, Places, and Objects** This poetry collection begins with an author's note, where Eloise Greenfield shares that her ideas come from memories of people and places, objects that she has and has observed, and her imagination. Before each poem, she describes her inspiration and where she got her writing idea.
What You Know First	Patricia MacLachlan	**Places** In this text, Patricia MacLachlan shows the reader just how sense of place fuels her writing. She writes of the many places that are important in Eli's (the character) life and how when writing, place provides us with ideas to write about.
A Box of Friends	Pam Muñoz Ryan	**Objects** In this text, Pam Muñoz Ryan creates a story about a grandmother who shows her grandchild precious objects in a box that remind her of the special people and memories from her life. To further support reluctant writers, ask them to create a box of objects that can serve as ideas for writing.
Best Wishes	Cynthia Rylant	**People, Places, Objects** In this autobiographical text, Cynthia Rylant points to all of her real-life inspirations for writing. She lets us know that she really did grow up in those mountains (place), that her son, Nate, and a big dog, Mudge, are the inspiration behind *Henry and Mudge* (people), and that her grandmother's kitchen table is where she always loves to be (object, place).
My Rotten Redheaded Older Brother	Patricia Polacco	**People** Patricia Polacco models how people are a great source for writing ideas, even when they are your pesky older brother!

Figure 8.2: Anchor Texts That Can Support Struggling Learners to Generate Writing Ideas

Figure 8.3: Welcome to My World Anchor Chart

Name: _____   Date: _____

My Writing Ideas

Figure 8.4: Writing Ideas Paper

Get Words on the Page Through Freewriting (3–8)

Sometimes, students who struggle with writing think they have nothing to write about or nothing to say about a topic or subject. We want our teaching to literally move them to a place of confidence and ideas. We can teach students specific and tangible strategies that will position them to feel they can easily compose writing by unlocking what they know.

In comes freewriting. What is freewriting? Sometimes called power writing (Fearn and Farnan 2001), freewriting is a brief, timed writing exercise that helps writers develop thinking and develop writing fluency. When freewriting, writers allow their thoughts to flow on paper, not censoring themselves in any way. It is about allowing thoughts to come to the page naturally, as opposed to second-guessing yourself and forcing ideas onto the page.

Why does freewriting support struggling learners? Because of the structure and nature of the strategy, students are freed from many obstacles they may have with writing, like getting going, getting graded, making mistakes, conventions, difficulty with disorganization or structure, and censoring themselves due to lack of confidence or other issues related to identity or self-efficacy.

How do you teach freewriting? Teaching any strategy involves defining the relevance, stating the rationale, and then modeling the strategy. You might say this:

> I've noticed that many of you are having trouble getting your writing going (or writing about a particular topic, etc.), so I want to show you a strategy that works for me. It is called freewriting. Freewriting is about freeing yourself from any difficulties or negative thoughts you have about writing and allowing yourself to just write. To begin, I may set up my page to remind myself what I want to write about. I do that by putting a title or idea box on the top of the page. I may choose to talk out my writing, in my own head or with another writer, before I get going. Either way, I set a goal to write for a set period of time. Let me show you what I mean. Today I will set the goal of writing for five minutes (or any length of time that you think will support your struggling students, such as between three and ten minutes). That means I will write and not lift my pencil from the paper (or fingers from the keyboard) for five straight minutes. Just start; just write. If you are not sure what to say, rewrite the last sentence you wrote, or write, "I do not know what to write next," until the next thought comes to you. Watch me.

It is as simple as that. Sometimes freewriting produces great writing. Sometimes it produces not so great writing. Both will happen, and both are okay. "The goal of freewriting is in the process, not the product" (Elbow 1981). By focusing on the process you provide struggling learners with a tangible strategy to unlock what they know.

#43 Rehearse Writing to Plan, Organize, and Brainstorm (K–8)

An important part of the writing process is rehearsal. Writers rehearse their writing before they write, and this can happen in different ways. For example, I sometimes dream my writing before I write, talk to a friend or writing partner, and even think about my writing in the shower. To me, rehearsal includes three essential elements of early writing: planning, organizing, and brainstorming. For our struggling students, rehearsal can help them perform these three tasks in tangible ways that will lead to success.

The goal of rehearsal is to provide the learner with an opportunity to think through ideas before she commits them to the page. The writer then takes the ideas and actually uses them to write. I see different rehearsal strategies used in the interest of supporting writers. However, these strategies are not always met with success. The issue is not with the rehearsal itself but with the type of rehearsal we are asking students to do. Moreover, we are not teaching them *how* and *when* to use a specific strategy and, more importantly, how to use the strategy to fuel the writing. Often I see struggling learners who believe that the rehearsal is the writing itself, or who will just copy the whole-class brainstorming chart onto their own page. Strategies are great, but they are only as effective as how well they are matched to the learner and to the context.

The writer does not rehearse writing and then leave those ideas behind; nor does the writer brainstorm ideas and then copy ideas exactly and precisely onto a piece of writing. A strong writer generates ideas about a topic and then uses what has been generated to write a piece. We want to equip our struggling writers to be strong in this area too!

Five rehearsal strategies work especially well with struggling writers: creating a memory window, creating an idea box, writing in the margins, writing in the air, and using storytelling. Some of the strategies help writers plan their writing, some help students organize their writing, some help students brainstorm and practice ideas, and some help students to do all three. Figure 8.5 shows what, where, how, and when you might use the five rehearsal strategies. Figures 8.6, and 8.7 are student examples of using an idea box and writing in the margins.

STRATEGIES FOR REHEARSING WRITING

REHEARSAL STRATEGY	WHAT THIS SUPPORTS	WHERE I MIGHT TEACH THIS	HOW TO IMPLEMENT THE STRATEGY	WHEN A STRUGGLING LEARNER MIGHT USE THIS STRATEGY
Creating a Memory Window	Plan, Brainstorm	Personal narrative, memoir, or reflections based an event, learning experience, trip, or activity	The writer creates a box and divides it into parts (three, four, or six work well). In each box, the writer tries to capture the memory/experience in some way. Some possibilities are: 1. Quick sketch 2. Describe the setting 3. Describe the light 4. Use any of the senses to describe the experience. 5. Write down words that describe how you felt. 6. Write similes or metaphors. 7. Write actions or interactions. 8. Write dialogue .	This strategy supports narrative or experiential writing. Unlike the web, this strategy allows the writer to attend to the idea in an organized or categorical way. It can also be adapted to specific learners because the box can contain anywhere from three to six parts. This strategy is good for learners who may have trouble remembering events or experiences, or learners who may struggle with using their brainstormed ideas.
Creating an Idea Box	Plan, Organize, Brainstorm	An idea box is an extremely versatile rehearsal strategy that can be used across content and genres including narrative, informational, procedural and opinion, or argument.	The writer creates a rectangular box on the top of the page. He will then proceed to put ideas in the box in a way that supports his task or purpose. An idea box can be used in: 1. Narrative: State the basic plot of a story, and then have bullets that outline the beginning, middle, and end. 2. Content Area—Science: State the experiment, and list the steps to the process or procedure. 3. Opinion/Argument: State a thesis (opinion or argument) and bullet reasons/parts and evidence that support that thesis. 4. Content Area—Math: State the answer or solution, and then list the steps taken to solve the problem.	This rehearsal strategy is perfect for planning, organizing, and brainstorming ideas and supports any type of writing. Unlike a graphic organizer, the benefit of the idea box is its direct proximity to the writing itself: The idea box is created on the top of the page rather than on another page. This strategy is good for struggling learners who may have trouble organizing their ideas and those who benefit from consistency and may have trouble managing different strategies used for different genres and contexts.

(continues)

Figure 8.5: Five Rehearsal Strategies

Figure 8.5 *(continued)*

REHEARSAL STRATEGY	WHAT THIS SUPPORTS	WHERE I MIGHT TEACH THIS	HOW TO IMPLEMENT THE STRATEGY	WHEN A STRUGGLING LEARNER MIGHT USE THIS STRATEGY
Writing in the Margins	Plan, Organize	Sequential writing including narratives, arguments, procedures, and essays	The writer jots ideas in the margin. These words and thoughts will serve as a reminder of what the writer wants to include in the piece. The writer jots the ideas in the margin, down the page in approximately the place the idea may go in the piece. If the strategy is being used to revise or add to writing, the writer rereads, makes notes, asks a question, and jots these down. The strategy can push the writer to stretch the writing and add more.	This rehearsal strategy supports writers who struggle with using their brainstorming ideas in their actual draft/writing, or writers who have trouble sequencing their writing. Like the idea box strategy, these generated ideas are put in direct proximity to the future writing, in approximately the place they will be used.
Writing in the Air	Brainstorm	Writing in the air is an extremely versatile brainstorming strategy that can be used across genres and content areas.	Either alone or with a partner, the writer shares ideas about her topic out loud. She can write in the air using general ideas (My story is about the moment I knew that Rosco would be my dog) or can be ideas that are specific. For example, the writer is working on crafting a lead, and she writes in the air what she might write. For example, I would say, "You are starting your piece by setting the scene. How might that go? Write in the air." The writer would then say, "I walked into Shake a Paw and could hear the sounds of excited puppies—barking, yelping, scratching, playing with toys. It was evening . . ." and would then proceed to jot down what was stated.	Writing in the air is about using oral rehearsal to fuel writing. Why do I call it writing in the air? Well, by calling it writing in the air, I am making a stronger connection from the brainstorming to the writing. I say to struggling writers, "Write in the air, then write on the page." It makes the actions seem like they go together. Plus, once you "write in the air," writing on the page does not seem so hard! Learners can even point to the page as they rehearse the writing, literally pointing to the part of the page where the writing will go.
Use Storytelling to Elaborate or Get Writing Going.	Plan, Brainstorm	Personal narrative; memoir; reflections from an event, learning experience, trip, or activity; anecdote used to fuel and support informational/ expository or opinion/ argument writing	Writers storytell using the following steps: • Think through the story, event, or part • Tell it to yourself • Tell it to others and get feedback • Tell it again after considering feedback.	A great time to use storytelling is during the generating, drafting, and revision stages. If writers want to generate or draft writing, have them tell stories in small group circles with feedback as part of the process. If writers are using storytelling to revise, suggest they tell their story with an angle in mind. They might focus on the "heart" of the story, the problem, or the lesson. Have them slow down this part as they storytell it to others. Peers listen and give feedback based on whether the problem or lesson was clear.

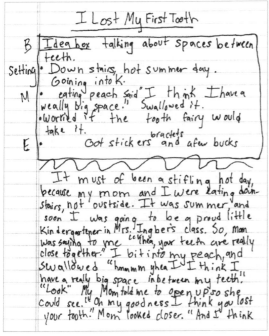

Figure 8.6: Using an Idea Box

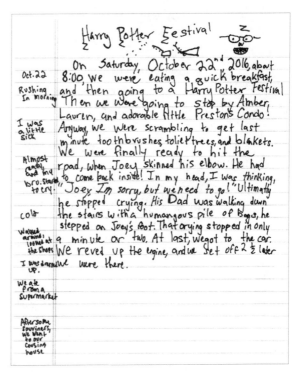

Figure 8.7: Writing in the Margins

#44 Use What They Know to Revise (3–8)

Let's face it, one of the most consistent ways learners struggle with writing is when they have to revise their writing to develop and elaborate on their ideas. Having moves that support writing development will go a long way.

The best way to teach students to develop their writing is to teach them strategies that allow them to use what they have and what they know to stretch the writing. Three developing strategies that do just that are *lift a line, box and jot,* and *write/sketch/write.*

LIFT A LINE IS A TANGIBLE STRATEGY BECAUSE THE WRITER IS LITERALLY AND IN TACTILE WAYS MANIPULATING HIS OR HER OWN WRITING.

When using *lift a line*, a writer goes back into the writing and lifts (almost physically, by copying a line from the page) a previously written line and uses that to continue writing. I first teach writers to find a part to lift and then teach them what to do after they lift a part out.

This benefits struggling writers for two reasons. First, writers can manipulate multiple parts of their writing. It is hard to "add in" to writing; however, if I lift it out, I can add on. Next, the strategy provides a context for learners to use what they think and what they know. Lifted lines can be copied onto a new page, scribed on a lined sticky note, or even written on a sentence strip. Students take the lifted line, elaborate, and write more. Figure 8.8 shows why and how students might lift a line. Figures 8.9a and 8.9b are examples of *lift a line*. Middle school writer James is lifting two lines in his multipage short story. After lifting the two lines, he stretches out the scene with description in one part and with dialogue in the other.

LINES OR PARTS TO LIFT	WHAT STUDENTS CAN DO WITH LIFTED LINES
An unclear sentence	Clear it up! Talk it out, then write it again.
An unfinished thought/an undeveloped part	Most often, I ask struggling writers to lift a line in an underdeveloped part of their writing. This could be a narrative scene that goes by too quickly or is not developed, a part of a poem with no imagery or detail, a section of informational text that requires explanation or some facts or graphics to illustrate the point, or even a section of an argument that needs more evidence to persuade or argue the claim. Lift it, and slow it down. Stretch it out by saying more and/or include details (actions, dialogue, feelings, descriptions, evidence) you forgot to include.
A part that confuses another writer	Lift parts where other writers have questions. Start by reading a piece to another writer. Note where he or she has questions. Lift those parts, and answer those questions. Add the detail, explanation, evidence, or thinking that will clear up the confusion.

Figure 8.8: How to Use *Lift a Line*

James   One Player Short

I wasn't really listening until coach said the word *quarterback*. I looked at the kid. He had blonde hair and was very tall, about 5'8". We went to our positions that we were going for this year. I was in the tryout with the same two kids as last year. "I am probably going to be the starting running back again," I thought to myself. I started to watch Joe during the tryout. After two hours the coach blew the whistle, which would mean to bring it in, and that practice was over. Coach talked about practice and said that there will be practice tomorrow at the same time. After practice I went up to Joe and said, "Good practice today," and stuck out my hand for a handshake.

    He stared at me and then looked down at my hand and shook it and said, "Thanks. You too."

Figure 8.9a: A section of James' writing before he used the strategy *Lift a Line*

Lift a Line, **Part 1:**

I started to watch Joe during the tryout. This kid had an arm and a half! He could throw accurate for about 50 yards, he could scramble in the pocket, and he could run. I knew that with this kid, we could win the national championship.

Lift a Line, **Part 2:**

After practice I went up to Joe and said, "Good practice today," and stuck out my hand for a handshake.

He stared at me and then looked down at my hand and shook it and said, "Thanks. You too."

"So, how did you like practice?" I asked.

"I really liked it. I liked the coach and the kids," he answered as he was putting his helmet and shoulder pads in his bag.

"We're going to win the national championship this year with you on our team," I said as I started to walk to my dad's car.

He put his head down, "I might not play with you guys this year," he said. "I might play with the San Francisco Titans instead."

My heart sank like I just got shot. My mouth dropped. My voice was hurting. "Oh," I said in a dinky voice.

Figure 8.9b: *Lift a Line*

Lift a line can be used in any genre but works particularly well in developing:

- Notebook entries
- Personal or fictional narratives
- Articles
- Speeches/debates
- Poetry
- Lab reports

BOX AND JOT PROVIDES WRITERS WITH AN ACCESSIBLE WAY TO INTERACT WITH MULTIPLE PARTS OF THEIR WRITING.

Box and jot asks a writer to do just that—reread their writing, and create a box around the parts that need revision. Students may box a part where they left out something they meant to include and will elaborate on that part with a few sentences. They may box a part and attend to word choice, replacing words with other words that are more precise, colorful, or indicative of the genre. They may even box a part and recraft it by adding dialogue, feelings, quotes, and explanations in a way that will enhance the writing. The jotting, which can be characterized as writing down phrases and parts that add to or enhance the writing, enables learners "add to" multiple parts of the piece. Before they jot in writing, students can jot verbally to get their thinking going. They box, jot verbally, and then write. They can repeat this process multiple times. See Figure 8.10 for an example of *Box and Jot*.

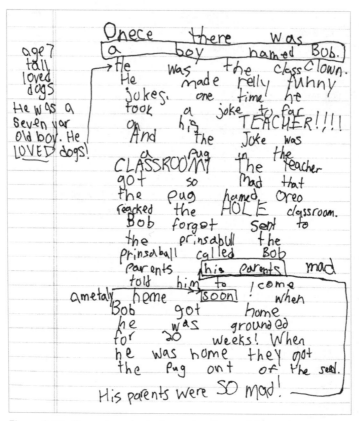

Figure 8.10: Second-grade student using *Box and Jot*

Box and jot can be used in any genre, but it works especially well in developing:

- Personal narratives
- Reviews
- Essays
- Question-and-answer books
- Research projects
- Lab reports

WRITE, SKETCH, WRITE IS ANOTHER STRATEGY THAT CAN HELP WRITERS TO REVISE THEIR WRITING. IT INCORPORATES ANOTHER MEDIUM INTO THE PROCESS.

Write, sketch, write, sometimes called *sketch to stretch*, is when writers use visual images to support more writing.

When you teach this strategy to struggling students, return to previous writing, sketch a visual image (that prompts further writing), and then use that sketch to write more. Students can sketch to add sensory details, show meaning, explain thinking, or reveal new thinking. *Write, sketch, write* can be used in any genre, but it works especially well in developing:

- Scenes in personal narrative/memoir/fictional narrative
- Reflections
- Explanations in articles or essays
- Summaries
- How-to texts

#45 *Create Opportunities for Feedback (K–8)*

We know how important feedback is in the writing process. We provide feedback in the form of written response, rubrics, and one-on-one conferences.

As a classroom teacher, I used both whole-class and partner structures to provide writing feedback. Many teachers use writing partnerships with their students, but they envision the partnerships as a mentoring model. In other words, "stronger" writers help students in need of support. It is fine to envision how one writer can mentor another, but I believe all writers can support each other by providing feedback. A few options follow.

SITTING IN THE CHAIR (WHOLE CLASS)

One writer sits before the writing community to receive feedback. The steps follow:

1. The writer signs up for feedback from our community. Prior to the feedback session, the writer must decide on a focus for the feedback—clarity, realistic dialogue, setting, leads, quality or quantity of evidence, and so on.

2. When the feedback session starts, the writer lets the group know what to focus on. The writer reads aloud a relevant a portion of the writing while it is projected in some way (document camera, Smart Board, copies for the class).

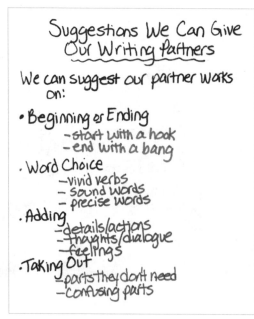

Figure 8.11: Suggestions for Writers Chart

3. Peers follow a protocol for providing specific positive and constructive feedback for the writer. I use the simple protocol of providing a "glow" and a "grow" to each writer. A glow is a compliment or strength in the writing. A grow is a place where the writing can be enhanced or revised.

4. The writer commits to trying at least one element of feedback in his or her writing.

5. End the feedback session by asking the rest of the class, "What feedback was given today that you can try in your own writing?"

Before you start the whole-class structure of "sitting in a chair," make sure to model how to find a part of your writing that needs feedback, how to provide constructive feedback, and refer back to (or create) anchor charts with writing advice or strategies (e.g., Suggestions for Writers Chart in Figure 8.11).

PEER CONFERENCE (PARTNERSHIPS)

The partnership structure has a similar protocol. Students should change partners routinely (for example, a new partner for each unit of study or quarter). Peer conferences are not discipline specific. Partners can give feedback on written material for any subject matter. I use this strategy with writers from early childhood through grad school. In fact, I recently used this strategy in a kindergarten one day, and in an AP language class the next day, with just a few modifications geared to the age of the students. Here are the steps for a partnership structure:

1. When a student wants feedback on a piece of writing (writing piece, lab summary, historical essay, and so forth), he asks his partner. The peer feedback conference would start just the way a whole-class protocol starts: with the student asking for something specific and then reading aloud a relevant portion of the writing.

2. The partner listens, names something positive about the writing, and provides constructive feedback.

3. The writer commits to trying at least one idea from the conference in his writing.

4. In both the whole-class and partnership structures, all students have the opportunity to both give and receive feedback.

Figure 8.12: Partner Protocol Chart

Figure 8.13: Picture of Feedback Clipboards

The following tools can scaffold the feedback experience so that it stays positive and effective for all:

- Suggestions for Writers Chart. This can be on a flip chart, Smart Board or other projection device but also works well if it is in Google Classroom for easy access (see Figure 8.11).

- An anchor chart of the partnership protocol. See Figure 8.12 for an example of a Partner Protocol Chart. This should be housed in the environment as an anchor chart but should also be given to students as individual copies.

- Clipboards or other materials to support the process. My colleague, Alisa Kadus, keeps clipboards with the partnership protocol in her writing center. She has two writer clipboards and two partner clipboards with the process taped onto them (see Figure 8.13).

#46 *Scaffold Through Paper Choice and Tools (K–2)*

I am definitely a field-of-dreams kind of teacher—if you build it, it will come—and this is no different for the teaching of writing. One of my favorite ways to support our youngest writers (and those with the least proficiency as writers) is to provide them with paper choice that will scaffold and support their work.

So how does paper choice support struggling learners? It scaffolds their writing development because you angle instruction and support around the format of the paper.

For example, for units in any discipline, decide what paper choices students will have. Then, *teach into* the paper choice and how each format can serve the writer. Figure 8.14 shows some paper choice options across genre and discipline.

When we angle paper choice toward the moves we want our struggling learners to make, we provide them with the scaffolding tools that will allow them to create and succeed!

PAPER CHOICE OPTIONS

GENRE	PAPER TYPES	ADDITIONAL PAPER/TOOLS
Narrative Writing	• Story paper with different lines (one line, three lines, five lines) that are structured both horizontally and vertically • Premade books of three to five pages with the words *beginning*, *middle*, and *end* on the bottom-right corner	• Premade speech bubbles • Story paper with thought bubbles • Premade books of 3, 5, or 7 pages
Informational Writing	• Informational paper of different formats including space for headings, questions, graphic aides, and special pages • Article format paper	• Premade glossary or picture-word list paper • Premade zoom boxes (circles, squares, rectangles that can include diagrams, fact boxes, and close-up pictures) • Research paper
Opinion Writing	• Story paper with different lines (one line, three lines, five lines) • Premade books of three to five pages with the words *topic/opinion*, *reasons*, and *powerful ending* on the bottom-right corner	• Planning/revision paper to generate reasons. Paper has first reason, second reason, third reason on it.
Any Genre	• Paper for special pages of a published book • Paper with borders, circles for page numbers, large lines for print • Half-pages of paper with lines to support revision, or adding on print or whole sections of writing	• Special pages for publishing including: about the author, title page, table of contents • Individual word wall with a personalized list of high-frequency words • Editing checklists that can be used by writing partners • Rectangle cutouts that students can use to find parts of their story where they can zoom in • Revision paper, including: lift-a-line paper, zoom-in paper, first try, second try, third try

Figure 8.14: Paper Choice Options Across Genre and Discipline

KEEP IN MIND

Sometimes we teach struggling learners formulaic and inauthentic strategies. We go for the popular culture acronym or the easy procedure to simplify what feels difficult. This does not actually help struggling learners *in the long run*. In our quest to provide students with tangible techniques, we oversimplify things and reduce writing to something it is not. So, here is what we ***don't*** want to do:

Lower expectations for length. Struggling learners are struggling; they are not incapable. Provide support, but do not require that they produce less writing. Lowering expectations can have a negative effect on learners, as they can develop issues of self-efficacy in addition to any content struggle.

Lower expectations for content or thinking. Struggling students may be struggling with the fundamentals of writing, but they do not, ever, have less to say. They have as many ideas, experiences, thoughts, and opinions as their peers. Our goal is to incorporate instructional moves that will support them but not diminish their content or thinking.

Teach inauthentic strategies. Mnemonics and acronyms are fine as reminders, but try not to reduce writing to something it is not. Find tangible ways to explain structure or craft (or whatever it is you are trying to simplify), but do not teach writers anything you wouldn't use or do yourself as a writer.

Instead we **want** to:

Have high expectations for all students. If we expect that our students write a certain amount each day, have the same expectations for our struggling students. To bridge the gap, teach them stamina strategies such as "write to the X" (a predetermined spot on their page that is typically more than what they will write in a day), or allow them to temporarily skip lines or start with a sketch to produce quantity in addition to quality.

Assume all students have something to say. Operate on the belief that we all have a story, we all have strong feelings and opinions, and we all have information to share and something we can teach others. When we start from this belief, we position ourselves to be primed to teach strategies that help struggling students move past any obstacles in writing without diminishing the content of their thinking.

Teach strategies that writers use. All writers get stuck, but good writers get unstuck. I share this with writers all the time, and in essence, by doing so, I show students that all of us struggle with our writing at some point in time. To move to a place where we can get unstuck, I teach students the strategies that I use as a writer, or that I have studied and noted in other writers. Authenticity matters, but it especially matters with struggling students. See Figure 8.15 for a class chart of strategies students can use if they are stuck.

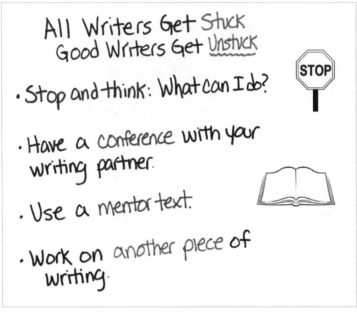

Figure 8.15: Ways to Get Unstuck

CHAPTER NINE

*H*ome Support

I hung up the phone and had to take a moment to process the conversation I just had. On the one hand I was ecstatic that I set up weekly check-ins with James's parents. On the other hand, I was amazed by what the conversations were revealing.

James was in the process of being evaluated for a learning disability. I knew that many subjects were hard for him and that he was having a particularly tough time in science. When his mom told me that he couldn't articulate the topic we'd just started studying in science, I knew I had to make some changes about how to support him.

Although it can sometimes feel hard, communication with parents and caregivers is important to student success. And when we are talking about struggling learners, home-school connections are a lifeline.

In "A New Wave of Evidence: The Impact of School, Family, and Community Connections on Student Achievement," authors Henderson and Mapp (2002) outline the reasons why strong home-school connections are so crucial to struggling learner success. They state:

> The evidence is consistent, positive, and convincing: families have a major influence on their children's achievement in school and through life. This fourth edition of *Evidence* confirms that the research continues to grow and build an ever-strengthening case. When schools, families, and community groups work together to support learning, children tend to do better in school, stay in school longer, and like school more.

How are the many ways in which families are engaged in their children's education related to achievement? Many studies found that students with involved parents, no matter what their income or background, were more likely to:

- Earn higher grades and test scores, and enroll in higher-level programs
- Be promoted, pass their classes, and earn credits
- Attend school regularly
- Have better social skills, show improved behavior, and adapt well to school
- Graduate and go on to postsecondary education (Henderson and Mapp 2002).

We can support our struggling learners by establishing effective home-school connections. Here are some tried and true ways to communicate with parents and caregivers.

#47 Establish Communication Protocols and Communicate Often (K–8)

Communicate with parents, and communicate often. Be proactive. Don't wait for parent-teacher conference night or a negative incident to occur, and don't let the first report card be your initial communication with parents. Here are some ways to establish communication protocols early on:

- Try to communicate with families before the school year begins. Send a letter or email home to the student and another one to caregivers, opening the doors of communication. The goal is not to set academic expectations but to open the lines of communication. In the parent letter I briefly introduce myself to the parents (*My name is Patricia Vitale-Reilly, and I am honored to be your child's _____ teacher this year.*). I say a little something about myself, and I usually include something professional and personal (*I have been in education for twenty-seven years and have two children of my own. My daughter, Rhiannon, will be a senior in high school this year, and my son, Jack, will be in eighth grade.*). I provide some options for how we can communicate this year (*I believe that consistent communication is key to supporting your child this year, and the best way to reach me is…*). Finally, I invite them to share with me any information that they want to about their child (*I am looking forward to getting to know your child. If there is anything you want me to know about your child, please feel free to reach out to me with this information. This can include your child's strengths, likes and dislikes, challenges, or something you are both proud of. If so desired, include a "selfie" of your family!*). I purposefully keep it simple. The intent of this communication is to build a relationship with each family, make them feel welcomed by honoring and acknowledging the information they have about their child, and provide families with ways that we can communicate about their child.

- Make sure you have a system for ongoing communication. In today's world, this is easier than ever. Communication can occur via email, a note home, text message, class website, or even social media. The key is to find the method and frequency that will work best for you and your families. Sometimes, texting can be the easiest way to communicate with families. Renee was struggling with how best to communicate with the family of a child who was having some challenges in school. The parent was extremely busy; she was working two jobs and had multiple family members she was caring for. Renee reached out to the parent using the contact information she had, including sending a text message. The parent responded right away and was so happy to have text messaging as a method of communication. They even worked out a routine so the parent would text Monday mornings to communicate any information she thought the teacher should know about the weekend. In turn, Renee would text on Fridays to communicate any information the parent should know about the week. Parents appreciate even a quick sentence or phrase to acknowledge a good week.

- Make sure to communicate with the parents of struggling students on an on-going basis. The goal is to be proactive. Communicate strengths, successes, and ways parents can support their child. If you have to communicate a struggle or an issue, you've already established a positive relationship. Take the time to have a positive exchange early in the year. For example, this past year I sent a quick email to Seth's parents letting them know how much I appreciated his eagerness to participate in class, as well as his thoughtful contributions (all true!). This made a more difficult communication go smoothly. I called his parents to discuss his constant interruptions and his struggle with one of our humanities chapters. We already had a rapport. His parents knew I appreciated Seth's strengths, and when it came time to discuss challenges, they respected the fact that my goal—*our* goal—was to support him. Our communications were always positive and fruitful. Ultimately, they helped Seth.

If your school has an online communication/grading system, be sure to use this tool wisely. Remind parents that it is there (I know, I know, they should know this already, but reminders go a long way!), and use it to help parents and students manage workload and success. Be sure to communicate any missing assignments, but also use it to acknowledge the effort that students are making. For example, consider adding a grade for effort into your repertoire of assessments. Post the effort grade in your online system at a midpoint to the quarter or on a monthly basis.

If your school does not have an online communication system (and even if it does), you might want to consider using Remind (www.remind.com). Remind is an online tool that allows you to send real-time messages to students and parents, individually or in groups. Text messages are sent without sharing a phone number and can be used to respond, remind, encourage, report, or continue class conversations. And the best part . . . it is free!

#48 *Make the Most Out of Back-to-School Nights (K–8)*

While back-to-school night is not a good time to go into detail about individual students, it is a great time to open and build communication. In addition to the structures you have in place for back-to-school nights, provide parents with pertinent and practical resources. Two great resources specifically tailored to supporting the families of struggling learners follow:

1. Mindprint Learning (https://mindprintlearning.com). Mindprint Learning is an online resource created by and for parents. A parent can use Mindprint for free by signing up for their toolbox through which they can access hundreds of strategies, resource reviews, and suggestions for classroom support for their child. Or, parents can subscribe to Mindprint and utilize the array of resources available. The first resource is an online diagnostic tool that students can take in the privacy of their own home in about an hour. After a student takes this assessment, Mindprint provides parents with a report detailing the strengths and needs of their learner, as well as suggestions for home and school learning. And last, a subscription to Mindprint provides parents with a personalized toolbox, curated according to the diagnostic assessment. The resources are geared toward not only students with learning disabilities but students who may struggle with learning for a variety of reasons. Plus, the folks at Mindprint are parents who have been there. They are so welcoming and willing to support the parents of any child who is experiencing struggles with his or her learning.

2. Understood.org (www.understood.org). Understood.org is a program offered through the National Center for Learning Disabilities. It combines the resources of fifteen nonprofits and is dedicated to supporting students who struggle with

learning and attention issues and their families. Their mission statement reads, "Our goal is to help the millions of parents whose children, ages 3–20, are struggling with learning and attention issues. We want to empower them to understand their children's issues and relate to their experiences. With this knowledge, parents can make effective choices that propel their children from simply coping to truly thriving." On the website, parents can find information about supporting struggling learners, navigating learning issues in school and at home, their child's rights, treatments and approaches to a variety of learning differences, and community events and groups. One of my favorite features is the parent toolkit. Here, parents can simulate a learning situation similar to their child's, get advice from a parenting coach, or find a variety of tech resources.

#49 Help Parents and Caregivers Understand Their Child as a Learner (K–8)

Parents and caregivers have an enormous amount of information about their child, so it's helpful to tap into their knowledge. I also want to provide parents with a tool that can help them build a student profile with what they know. This will enable us to support their child both in school and at home. Start with the questionnaire in Figure 9.1.

STUDENT PROFILE QUESTIONNAIRE

The following questionnaire is categorized using four learner attributes crucial for student success: engagement, perseverance, retention of learning, and adaptability. Each, in its own way, contributes to a successful year of learning.

Each attribute is defined. After the definition are a series of questions. Please note, I have referred to your child as "the learner" so that each of us can fill out this form. Please answer the questions as honestly as you can. Together we will use the information to support your child at home and in school.

I. Engagement

Engagement is defined as being invested, involved, and absorbed in a task or endeavor. Learners can show engagement in a variety of ways, including through interest, participation, initiative, stamina, or commitment.

- Is the learner actively involved in his learning life? Does he advocate for and initiate his own learning?

Figure 9.1: Student Profile Questionnaire

(continues)

© 2018 by Patricia Vitale-Reilly from *Supporting Struggling Learners*. Portsmouth, NH: Heinemann.

Figure 9.1   *(continued)*

- Is the learner interested in learning? Can you identify subjects and topics by which the learner is interested or excited?

- Does the learner disconnect during learning? If so, when does this happen? If so, do you see any effect on learning such as loss of interest, less stamina, lack of task completion, or lack of understanding?

II. Perseverance

Perseverance is defined as having purpose, resolve, and stick-to-itiveness. Successful students persevere through a variety of teaching and learning contexts including challenging texts, long assignments and tasks, detailed or multistep directions, and long-term projects.

- Does the learner exhibit stamina for learning? If so, when? Is this discipline/task-specific?

- What does the learner do when stuck? Does the learner have any strategies for working through difficulties?

- Can the learner manage frustration? Whether yes or no, please provide specific examples.

III. Retention of Learning

Retention of learning is the ability to remember what has been taught. The learner may need to recall the information the next day, the next week or unit, or even after a longer period of time such as the next year.

- Does the learner retain what has been taught? Can he say back what he has learned?

- Does this differ in different contexts? Do you notice that size of group or method of instruction (such as use of technology or kinesthetic experiences) matters? Provide specific examples.

- What, if anything, helps the learner to retain information?

(continues)

Figure 9.1 *(continued)*

- Does the learner retain learning in a particular discipline (including a sport, hobby, or interest inside or outside of school)?

IV. Adaptability

Adaptability is the ability to be flexible or change or adjust direction, mood, or idea based on context or need.

- Can the learner adapt to new situations and routines with appropriate notice and transition time?

- When does the learner seem least adaptable? Most adaptable?

Student's Name_____ Your Name _____

You may need to offer parents alternatives to a written questionnaire. Some parents might prefer to answer your questions over the phone or during a face-to-face meeting. If you need translation services, seek help from your principal or district.

Once you complete the questionnaire and receive a completed questionnaire from parents, compare the information. What do you notice? Are there patterns or similarities in your response? Are there places where your responses differ greatly? Do any responses surprise you? Do you need to follow up and get more information? Once you've gathered enough information, make recommendations to parents about how to support their child. Break it down by the categories in the questionnaire. Figure 9.2 gives you examples of suggestions you might give to parents about how they can support their learner at home:

SUGGESTIONS BASED ON STUDENT PROFILE QUESTIONNAIRE

Thank you for filling out the Student Profile Questionnaire. Based on both of our responses, I suggest the following as ways we can support your child. Feel free to implement any of the suggestions below; however, I have highlighted the suggestions that I think will work well for your learner.

I. Engagement

- Provide your child with the opportunity to have a say in his or her own learning. Let the child decide what part of homework he or she wants to start first, or if he or she wants to have a snack before or after. Allow your child to practice decision-making regarding his or her own home learning. Starting with small decision-making steps will lead to greater initiative.

Figure 9.2: Suggestions Based on Student Profile Questionnaire

(continues)

Figure 9.2   *(continued)*

- Bring your child's interests into the learning experience. For example, Max's mother frequently changes the names of the people in math problems to the names of family members and friends, and John's dad spends time each week with him as he chooses his independent reading texts. Both John and his dad tend to like reading about sports, from sports fiction to the sports section in the newspaper, and choosing interesting texts together has increased John's engagement in reading.

- Maintain a strong relationship with your child's teacher. Commit to a weekly communication protocol. Engagement increases when your child knows you communicate with the teacher on a regular basis.

II. Perseverance

- Set a schedule and calendar for tasks. Include home reading, homework, and chores such as setting the table or walking the dog. Display the schedule so there is a visual reminder. Make sure the tasks are set in manageable chunks so your child does not become overwhelmed.

- Allow your child to take breaks. We build stamina and our ability to persevere when we gently and incrementally boost the amount of time we spend on tasks.

- Encourage your child to seek help when something feels challenging. Brainstorm different ways your child can seek help, such as the following:

  ▸ Phone a friend: Encourage your child to call a friend who might be able to help.
  ▸ Ask a family member for help: a sibling, parent or guardian.
  ▸ Jot a note for the teacher: Be sure to explain what is working, and where you got stuck.
  ▸ Get help from a kid-friendly search engine: Try kidrex, www.kidrex.org; Wonderopolis, www.wonderopolis.org; and kidzsearch, www.kidzsearch.com.

III. Retention of Learning

- Access the class website with your child for information about current units of study. The more information you have about what is being taught, the more you'll be able to reinforce what is happening at school.

- Ask questions to help your child hold on to learning. If you know what your child is studying, ask specific content questions like: What are you learning about fractions this week? What is the most interesting thing you have learned about ocean animals? What are you writing about? What book are you reading? Ask the questions casually, as you would in a friendly conversation, and maintain a genuine interest. This will engage the student in an authentic exchange, something that will support retention of ideas. It is certainly better than the old, how was school today?

- Establish a guidance protocol. A guidance protocol should support your child during home study. A guidance protocol is not just about the what of the homework but is about creating a supportive process for your child. You might ask the following questions to support home assignments:

  ▸ What is your assignment?
  ▸ What do you need to do the assignment?
  ▸ How will you start?
  ▸ How will you finish?

(continues)

Figure 9.2 *(continued)*

IV. Adaptability

- Model adaptability for your child. One way you can do that is to talk about moments in your day when you had to adapt. Think about a moment in your personal or workday when you had to change or shift your task, routine, or perspective. Describe the moment, and follow up by sharing how you felt when you had to shift gears. Make sure to point out the benefits of being adaptable.

- Build in transition time. Changing on a dime is hard for many people so when your child needs to shift gears, explain the change and provide transition time. Transition time allows your child to mentally prepare for the change.

#50 *Help Parents Create Supportive Home Environments (K-8)*

Since learning happens at home and school, it is important to discuss the home environment with parents. A home can be a busy, noisy place, an environment that more often than not does not work for struggling learners. Therefore, consider providing parents with specific tips that can support their struggling learner at home.

Tip #1: **Create a space for studying and reading.** You do not have to have an extra room to implement this tip. You can create a designated reading and study space by using space that does double duty. For example, a clear dining room table (seldom used for family meals except for holidays) can be a calm, quiet space for homework or home reading. Or, consider purchasing a desk that can be used for homework or home reading. The child's bedroom might be a more conducive space for studying and reading,

Figure 9.3: A Portable Desk

away from the hustle and bustle of dinner preparation and other family activities. Or, create a study nook by purchasing a clipboard or plastic portable desk with side pockets (easily and inexpensively purchased at stores like Staples or Target) and create an "office" for homework and reading. Figure 9.3 illustrates this idea.

Tip #2: **Minimize distractions.** Turn off the TV, remove electronics, and encourage quiet conversations during homework or studying time. If you create a distraction-free zone in support of a struggling learner, home time will be more fruitful and much, much less stressful.

Tip #3: **Organize!** Organization has an impact on the success of homework and home reading. Organize school papers, homework, materials, and supplies. Have a designated spot for backpacks, shoes, and coats (such as hooks, shelves, benches), and expect that your child will put their belongings in that spot. Have a designated spot for any paper communication, like a basket, folder, or drawer. Require your child to save files, store the digital file, and/or put all materials back in the folder, file, or backpack in the evening. Cleaning up the night before helps avoid a stressful start to the school day. An organized home environment supports home study and greatly reduces stress or frustration.

KEEP IN MIND

Home visits are another effective form of communication with students and their parents or caregivers. Consider conducting home visits before the school year begins, or try to schedule them for early in the school year. You might add a section in your first letter offering families a choice about home visits. If they are interested in a home visit, make sure to give them options for days and times. While not all families will feel comfortable inviting you into their homes, you'll find that many families are eager to talk to their child's teacher in their home environment. Reassure families about the positive purpose of the home visit: to learn about their child's family, to gather information about their child's interests and strengths, and to give families a chance to share any relevant information in the privacy of their homes.

CHAPTER TEN

I_f... Then

So there you have it—fifty instructional moves that will help struggling learners navigate the terrain of your classroom in ways that will lead to success. There are always other issues or needs that impact teaching and learning. Here are three questions I'm asked most frequently:

1. What if the student needs more support?

2. How do I monitor a child's progress?

3. How can I make the most of my co-teacher or teacher's aide?

I'll try to answer these questions and provide you with tools and information (backed by research) to guide you on your journey:

1. *If* you need more support for your struggling learner, **then** you may want to use the protocol I provide to move through your school's child study team process.

2. *If* you need to progress-monitor a student—a learner you plan to bring to the child study team, a learner who has been to the child study team and is involved in an RtI (Response to Intervention) process, a special education student who has goals and objectives you need to monitor— **then** you want to use progress-monitoring tools that will make the process seamless, simple, and strong.

3. *If* you have the benefit of a co-teacher or a teacher's aide, **then** you will want to harness the power of two and use co-teaching models of instruction.

If You Need More Support

Let's face it, sometimes you've done everything you can think of in the classroom, but it doesn't feel like enough. Your learner might need the support of the larger school community. Most learning environments support a formal process for identifying the needs of students. In 2017, most schools follow some variation of an RtI protocol—that is, they start with a core curriculum and identify learners who are struggling with this curriculum. From there, an effective support protocol ***should*** include the following:

Tip *Reach out to your school support team to schedule time to discuss the struggling learner. Be sure to bring documentation of what you have noticed, what you have tried, the learners' strengths, and what you feel the learner is struggling with. See Figures 10.1 and 10.2 for tools you can use for this process.*

Tip *Be sure to ask a lot of questions and be very specific about what you have tried and what you haven't. It helps if you have documentation of prior moves. In addition, inquire about the composition of the child study team. They are filled with experts (e.g., psychologists, social workers, occupational therapists, and so on) with lots to offer in their specific fields. However, they may not have the expertise to provide interventions that will be pertinent to your struggling learner. If reading and math specialists are not a part of the school support team, perhaps you can request the addition of a reading specialist, math specialist, or special educator to the conversation so that the suggestions are actionable and individualized to the learner.*

- **Begin the process of further identifying what is getting in this learner's way.** This is an important first step you can take, and from here you can bring the information to your school's support team to build an intervention plan that will become an action plan for learning. The identification stage is key to the success of the intervention plan. In *Visible Learning: A Synthesis of Over 800 Meta-Analyses Relating to Achievement* (2009), John Hattie identified comprehensive interventions for learning disabilities as having .77 effect on student achievement. This translates to significant gains in learning for students who struggle. We know that comprehensive intervention plans begin by accurately and specifically identifying learning challenges and struggles, so let's begin here.

- **Teacher refers struggling student(s) to the school support team.** Each building has a team of support specialists who can help you navigate this process. This group has a different name in different schools/states (IST, CSE, I&RS, and so on), so for our purposes here, I will call this team a School Support team. A school support team is a group of professionals, chosen by the school, whose role is to provide a teacher with modifications for struggling students, recommendations for classroom interventions, recommendations for supplemental support, and, if applicable, a process to determine eligibility for special education testing. Speak to your principal about who is in this team and how to schedule time to meet with this team. You may need to fill out a form that asks you to explain why you are bringing the student to the team.

- **The school support team will recommend interventions and modifications to try.** After you meet with the school support team, they will make recommendations. You might find that the suggestions are general, not specific to a particular learner, or that the recommended interventions are ones you have already tried. If that is the case, ask questions, ask for specifics, or reach out to a building specialist (math, reading, or special educator) for support.

> **Tip** *Be open to the recommendations provided by the school support team, and really commit to trying them out. And most importantly, monitor what is happening. See Figure 10.8 for an easy-to-use record keeping form that will enable you to keep track of this information.*

- **The teacher implements suggested interventions, then monitors progress or lack thereof.** This step is crucial. It is here that you are really trying out interventions, modifications, and scaffolds to support the struggling learner.

- **The teacher and the school support team communicate regularly.** This step is important as time is of the essence when creating and implementing an intervention plan that will lead to learner success.

> **Tip** *Set a timely check-in goal (between four and eight weeks is ideal), and be sure to keep in touch with the school support team members between meetings. Ask questions, ask for support, or share success stories.*

- **Next steps are determined.** When you reconvene with the school support team, a decision will be made regarding next steps for this student. The team may determine that the interventions, modifications, or supports have worked. In this case, continue implementing the interventions, modifications, or supports, adjusting as necessary. The team may determine that the student needs supplemental support. In this case, be supportive of this additional instruction. Share information with the supplemental support teacher, and create a protocol for communication. Support the learner as he or she transitions to having additional instruction and time outside the classroom. The team may decide that the student needs to be assessed for a learning disability.

> **Tip** *In this case, support the learner, communicate with the parents, and support the process. Know when testing will occur, and be sure the student is clear on the process (as applicable based on the developmental needs and age level of the student).*

In all my work with classroom teachers and school support teams, I have seen examples of successful and not-so-successful team meetings. At the end of the successful meetings, teachers feel heard, team members feel accomplished and helpful, and, most importantly, everyone leaves with a solid plan of action (intervention plan) for the learner. To improve the chances of a successful outcome with your school support team meetings, use the suggestions in Figure 10.1.

SUGGESTION	SPECIFIC PLAN
Gather *specific* evidence of learning and learning struggles.	Gather assessments administered to the entire class and to the individual learner. Be sure to gather record-keeping documents and tools used with this learner. See Figure 10.2 for a list of possible assessments and record-keeping tools. Figures 10.3–10.14 serve as examples.
Prepare for the meeting.	Before the meeting gather data on the student, and read through your notes, assessments, observations, and so on. You might want to pare down the "evidence" that you are bringing to the meeting. In my experience three to five artifacts and specific points will provide enough information without overwhelming the team.
Speak clearly, specifically, and objectively about the student.	As teachers we are so connected to and passionate about our students. That said, it is best to speak to a school support team as objectively as you can. School support team members do best when they are presented with specific information—nouns and verbs and not descriptive qualifiers (lots of adjectives and adverbs) about a student. The more specific we are, the more we present an objective view of the learner.
Be this student's best advocate.	Although we want to be objective and specific, we do not want to be afraid to advocate for the student. Expect the school support team to offer suggestions and a plan of action that truly meets the needs of this learner. You might need to ask for specifics when suggestions are made and write down the exact plan of action. A good plan of action should include the plan, suggestions for interventions, modifications (if applicable), who is responsible for implementation, time frame, and next steps.

Figure 10.1: Suggestions for Improving the Chances of a Successful Outcome with Your School Support Team Meetings

---

POSSIBLE ASSESSMENTS TO GATHER AND
BRING TO A SCHOOL SUPPORT TEAM MEETING

Benchmark Reading Assessments

Examples include Fountas and Pinnell Benchmark Assessment, DRA, IRLA.

Performance Based Assessments

Examples include ELA, math, or content area performance tasks administered at the beginning or end of a unit or module.

Teacher Record Keeping - Notes from Conferences and Progress Monitoring

Examples include conferring notes, unit checklists representing learning goals, anecdotal records, specific progress monitoring forms or assessments.

Student Record Keeping

Examples include reading record, reading log, writing about reading, goals and plans forms, reflections rubrics.

Running Records with Comprehension Check

Running records can be from guided reading texts, independent reading texts, or cold reads.

Figure 10.2: Possible Assessments to Bring to Student Support Team Meetings

Navigating support, intervention, identification, and possible classification isn't easy, but if we understand the kind of learner a student is, and if we have a good process for communicating with specialists in our schools, our students are best positioned to receive the support that they need.

If You Need to Progress-Monitor a Student

It is sometimes challenging to quantify a learning struggle. As teachers, we have great instincts on how students learn. I value that, truly, and feel that my own teacher gut has led me to much success in supporting all learners. However, in our data-driven culture, great instincts, descriptions, and stories about learning aren't always enough. In addition, we want to avoid needlessly recommending students for special education services. It is best to think about how we can quantify our "gut" and experiences with students.

Tools such as learning checklists, observational record keeping geared toward progress monitoring, and class forms are all examples of tools that we as teachers can use to monitor learning and progress. The following are examples of tools that I have used to successfully communicate learning struggles and monitor any successes a student is experiencing.

STUDENT CHECKLISTS

Checklists can be used in all disciplines, from ELA to math to content areas during any time of the day or period. I typically find the most success using checklists in the following three ways:

1. First, you can use whole-class checklists. A whole-class checklist can be used to plan for whole-class instruction, but it can *also* serve as a record of progress made. For example, when planning for reading instruction, I frequently sit with student reading tools—a list of texts read/reading logs, response notebooks, student goals, unit goals, current texts with sticky notes, and other tools as well to monitor any progress and plan for instruction. When you sit side by side with the student tools you can see real evidence of learning and then use checklists to note progress or identify next instructional steps. Figure 10.3 is an example of a whole-class checklist that I used to plan lessons (whole-class and small-group) and capture and monitor progress both in a beginning-of-the-year reading unit of study as well as across the year.

2. Next, if you take the time to observe students during independent practice, really "reading the room," you can use a checklist to note student learning. Figure 10.4 is an also an example of a whole-class checklist that can monitor progress and plan for instruction. I use this checklist to monitor student conversations during partner, small-group, and whole-class conversations across the disciplines.

3. Last, during one-to-one student conferences and during small-group instruction, you will want to take notes on student learning. Using a checklist feels manageable for two reasons. One, the number of students you are taking notes on is reduced (one student, if this is during an individual conference, and at most five to six students in a small group). In addition, a checklist names the skills, strategies, and behaviors that you will need to be looking for and, therefore, makes record keeping simple and concrete. Figures 10.5, 10.6, and 10.7 are examples of student over time subject-specific checklists. "Student over time" indicates that this tool is for one student and is used to document successes, struggles, or challenges over a period of time. The length of time can be set (e.g., a unit of study) or over a period of time (e.g., a quarter or trimester). These reading and writing checklists can be used during independent practice, one-to-one conferences, or small-group instruction. When using a subject-specific checklist, I typically record the date and either an "S" to indicate specific evidence of successful learning or a "C" to note challenges with the skill or concept.

READING ENGAGEMENT CHECKLIST

Student	Identifies reading preferences; chooses books by purpose and interest	Tracks reading using reading log	Sets reading goals; is working toward goals	Sustains reading for ___ minutes	Uses strategies to preview a book	Shares ideas about a book	Participates in reading conferences	Notes

Figure 10.3: Reading Engagement Checklist

SPEAKING AND LISTENING CHECKLIST

Student	Demonstrates a listening stance	Participates during partner conversations	Participates in whole-class conversations	Shares: prediction/ hypothesis, connection, conclusion	Asks Qs	Answers Qs	Builds on comments of others	Notes

Figure 10.4: Speaking and Listening Checklist

STUDENT OVER TIME READING CHECKLIST

NAME:	READING LEVEL:	PROGRESS MONITORING:			
READING INDICATOR		Dates Observed/Notes S = strengths C = challenges TP = teaching point			
Reading Process, Behaviors, and Habits					
Selects books by: interest and purpose					
Selects book by genre: _____					
Sustains reading for _____ minutes					
Maintains focus and attention to page or partner					
Print and Fluency					
Flexibly uses strategies to read an unfamiliar a word					
• Recognizes high-frequency words					
• Uses word parts to solve new or multisyllabic words					
• Uses the structure of the sentence to solve words					
• Makes a guess and cross-checks using other strategies					
Demonstrates phrasing and fluency through stress, intonation, pausing, and expression.					
Comprehension					
Uses previewing strategies including looking at title, cover, blurb, author, genre, or content					
Monitors when meaning is lost					
Retells a text with supporting details					
Uses text features to read and locate information					
Uses comprehension strategies					
• Makes predictions					
• Makes connections and comparisons to texts					
• Infers ideas related to character or theme					
• Understands aspects of genre, structure, language, or craft					
• States opinions; understands opinions of others					
Notes:					

Figure 10.5: Student over Time Reading Checklist

NAME: Molly	READING LEVEL: P	PROGRESS MONITORING: Yes		
READING INDICATOR		**Dates Observed/Notes** **S = strengths** **C = challenges** **TP = teaching point**		
Reading Process, Behaviors, and Habits				
Demonstrates reading preferences; selects books by interest and purpose		9/10	9/18 S	
Selects book by genre: Mystery		9/10 S	9/18 S	
Reads regularly at home		9/14 S	9/21 S	9/28 S	10/5 S
Sustains reading for 15 minutes		9/12 S	9/17 S	9/27 C	
Maintains focus and attention to page or partner		9/21—partner			
Print and Fluency				
Flexibly uses strategies to read an unfamiliar a word				
• Recognizes high-frequency words				
• Uses word parts to solve new or multisyllabic words				
• Uses the structure of the sentence to solve words				
• Makes a guess and cross-checks using other strategies		9/18 uses in conf.		
Demonstrates phrasing and fluency through stress, intonation, pausing, and expression		9/18 shows in conf.		
Comprehension				
Uses previewing strategies including looking at title, cover, blurb, author, genre, or content		9/10 Conf. TP	C Prompt 9/18	C Prompt 9/25
Monitors when meaning is lost		C 9/18 conf. TP	S Using strategy 9/21	

Figure 10.6: Sample Student over Time Reading Checklist

(continues)

Figure 10.6 *(continued)*

NAME: Molly	READING LEVEL: P	PROGRESS MONITORING: Yes			
READING INDICATOR		**Dates Observed/Notes** **S = strengths** **C = challenges** **TP = teaching point**			
Reading Process, Behaviors, and Habits *(continued)*					
Retells a text with supporting details		C 9/18 conf.			
Uses text features to read and locate information					
Uses comprehension strategies					
• Makes predictions		S 9/14 whole class			
• Makes connections and comparisons to texts		9S /24 whole class			
• Infers ideas related to character or theme		C 9/27 Conf. TP			
• Understands aspects of genre, structure, language, or craft					
• States opinions; understands opinions of others		S 10/8 Conf. TP			

Notes: 9/10 conference, taught her to preview; needs prompting each time starts new book, 9/18 conference asked to read aloud page to me. Good cross-checking, fluency. Retelling was spotty—couldn't retell all important info, didn't use character names, wasn't sure where meaning broke down. TP monitoring by stopping at stopping points (we preplanned a few) to check understanding; go back to reread if lost. Also retell to partner at beginning of partner talk each day. 9/21—check-in, quick retell shows success; started partner talk this way. 9/27 conference: inferring ideas about character hard. Good hunches based on actions and descriptions of character. Once got into interactions, dialogue, or what other characters say, not able to infer. Taught her to slow down at dialogue and character-to-character parts—think, use what you know about life and other characters; infer. 10/8: excellent at forming opinions and listening to the opinions of others. Pushed her thinking by teaching her to show evidence and use text features or elements to support.

WRITING ENGAGEMENT CHECKLIST

WRITING ENGAGEMENT INDICATOR	DATES OBSERVED			
Writing Process, Behaviors, and Habits				
Gets started easily				
Writes with stamina (words on page) _____				
Writes with stamina (time writing) _____				
Uses strategies to sustain writing time _____				
Participates in writing conferences				
Generating Ideas				
Generates writing ideas				
Manages and uses writing tools to plan and generate				
Reflection				
Reflects on writing both process and output				
Identifies strengths and areas of growth				
Notes:				

© 2018 by Patricia Vitale-Reilly from *Supporting Struggling Learners*. Portsmouth, NH: Heinemann.

Figure 10.7: Writing Engagement Checklist

Checklists can be created for any and all disciplines. The key is to note what discipline-specific evidence you will be looking for and create a form that will be easy to manage and use during both instruction and planning.

CONFERENCE NOTES

Conference notes are a type of anecdotal record keeping that many teachers use in a variety of disciplines, for a variety of purposes. The note-taking form in Figure 10.8 is a conference form designed specifically for students who are struggling in any subject area, and are involved in an RtI process. In Figure 10.9 I share an example of when I used this form to monitor the progress of a student. It contains space to record the typical conference information (date, research, compliment, teaching point), but it is also designed to record and monitor any evidence of learning and progress. This is helpful in communicating when progress is lacking or slower than the rate of a typical developing learner. This information is important to understand for your own planning purposes but also important to communicate to parents, special educators, or school support team members so that specific interventions or supplemental support can be suggested. When using conference notes to progress-monitor students, it is imperative to record the following:

- Date. Progress monitoring requires more frequent observation and check-in on the learner.

- Research. This is where I note the gist of the conversation, indicating how I made a decision on the teaching point. The research can happen before the conference begins (see notes from 9/9 in Figure 10.9) and/or at the beginning of the conference.

- Compliment. In a strengths-based model, offering the learner a compliment—recognition of his or her competencies as a learner—will engage students and provide them with information on what they are doing well as a learner.

- Teaching Point. As obvious as it sounds, noting exactly what you taught is key to progress monitoring. What specific strategy, process, skill, or habit did you teach the learner? How did you do this? Noting this and then noting what is working and not working allows you to build a bank of successful teaching techniques you can later draw from.

- Observable Progress/Notes. This is the category that is different from many other conference forms. It's a space to record observable progress or lack thereof. This portion of the form helps you see what teaching is working. In addition, notes from this section contain information that is important to communicate to child study team members.

PROGRESS MONITORING CONFERENCE FORM

Name: _____

Date:

Research:

Compliment:

Teaching Point:

Observable Progress/Notes:

Date:

Research:

Compliment:

Teaching Point:

Observable Progress/Notes:

Date:

Research:

Compliment:

Teaching Point:

Observable Progress/Notes:

Date:

Research:

Compliment:

Teaching Point:

Observable Progress/Notes:

Figure 10.8: Progress Monitoring Conference Form

Name: Ryan

Date: 9/9

Research: Only student without an independent reading book. Noticed he had been browsing books and asking students. Spoke to librarian. Still no book.

Compliment: *I can see you tried many strategies to find a book.*

Teaching Point: Using what you know about yourself and the strategies you are trying to choose a text and stick with it. Identified three texts using his strategies. Talked through choices. Chose a Wayside book.

Observable Progress/Notes: Interesting to note that he appears to have strategies, but they do not pan out. Looks like he is going through the motions. Unable to use strategies as a means to an end.

Date: 9/20

Research: Still reading the Wayside book chosen in the previous conference but not very far along in the book. Asked him to read a portion to me to do a quick miscue and retelling. Three errors out of 100 words, and retell had appropriate parts including some details, character names, and text vocabulary. Text moving along slowly so addressing that.

Compliment: *I like how you are working your way through your text and say that you are enjoying it.*

Teaching Point: Pacing your reading. Find meaning chunks that are smaller than chapters. Pause to check-in to self, keep going. Together planned meaning/reading chunks.

Observable Progress/Notes: Ryan is sticking to his choice and reading with basic meaning (retelling to partner at end of workshop and to me in conference is solid), but reading is going very slow. Will check in on the TP from today to see if strategy on pacing is helping him.

Date: 9/23

Research: Observed him using the strategy we discussed during two of the three next days.

Compliment: *I can see you are mostly remembering to do what we talked about, and you are sticking with your book.*

Teaching Point: Just for the next week, using a log to record amount read. Take short breaks in reading to give yourself a breather, then keep reading to next meaning chunk. Can talk to partner in between as well.

Observable Progress/Notes: Strategies are utilized but needs reinforcement, prompting, reminders. Some issues with "stickability" of teaching points.

Figure 10.9: Student Sample of Progress Monitoring Conference Form

Figure 10.10 is another example of a progress monitoring conference form. However this one is organized into columns of information: student goal or objective, date, strategy used to achieve the goal, and evidence of progress/notes. This conference form allows you to take notes in an anecdotal way but is also preorganized and geared toward a specific goal. Figure 10.11 shows how I used this form with John.

PROGRESS MONITORING CONFERENCE FORM WITH GOALS AND STRATEGIES

Name _____

Goal for the Learner	Date	Strategy Implemented	Evidence of Progress/ Notes

Figure 10.10: Progress Monitoring Conference Form with Goals and Strategies

Name: John

Goal for the Learner	Date	Strategy Implemented	Evidence of Progress/ Notes
John will read texts up to 150 words with 95 percent accuracy.	1/23	Index card to track reading.	Used a nonlined colored index card, and that focused him for the entire text. Running record noted two errors in the 200-word passage.
John will identify when comprehension breaks down.	2/3	Verbal Prompts from Prompt Card: "Reading is no longer making sense."	John used one of his verbal prompts, "Reading is no longer making sense," but could not explain why or where the breakdown started. Going to provide John with tabs to mark when he feels the bird-walking happening and ask him to employ a two- or three-page stop and check.
John will recall and verbally state three details from a section of informational reading.	2/6	Talk to his reading partner illuminating important details.	John was able to share three details from a section of a science text. The headings were a great guide to help him navigate where the details came from and were used to remind him of what he was going to be reading about.
John will retell narrative chapters including the characters, setting, and plot.	2/11	Story elements bookmark	John is looking at the bookmark to remind himself of what needs to be included. He was able to include all elements, but the retell was random. Need to focus on order and what specifically to include.

Figure 10.11: Student Sample of Progress Monitoring Conference Form with Goals and Strategies

WHAT IS WORKING/WHAT IS NOT WORKING
CLASS-AT-A-GLANCE FORM

NAME	STRATEGY/ ACCOMMODATION	WORKING	NOT WORKING	NOTES

Figure 10.12: What Is Working/What Is Not Working: Class-at-a-Glance Form

The steps that I took to fill out the progress monitoring conference form were as follows:

1. Extract information on student outcomes (from an IEP, teacher/school support team written objectives, individual student goals, goals from a unit of study, and so on), and list in column 1: the Goal for the Learner column.

2. Decide when the recordings will occur. They might be at predetermined junctures (a specific day of the week, or during conferences), naturally as teaching occurs, or a combination of both.

3. Decide on a time frame for this progress monitoring. Optimal time frame is between two and six weeks.

CLASS FORMS

Let's admit it, progress monitoring can feel challenging when combined with all the other data gathering we do on our students. If this describes you, then you will want to try class forms. Class forms are just that—record keeping that is organized as a "class-at-a-glance" tool. When I use the term "class-at-a-glance," what I mean is that you can see your entire class (or as many learners as you want to see at a time) on the page. Figure 10.12 is an example of a class form, organized by the categories of what is working and what is not. Figure 10.13 is an example filled out.

Of course, any class form can become a student over time form, and if you find that one student needs more frequent and detailed record keeping and progress monitoring, then you can easily change a class form into a student over time form. Figure 10.14 is an example of this for one student, Alex, in math.

Teacher _____				
NAME	**STRATEGY/ ACCOMMODATION**	**WORKING**	**NOT WORKING**	**NOTES**
Emma	Formula card		X	Not keeping track of formula cards, so not accessing.
Samir	Sticky note prompts	X		Using when needed and ground him in the task. Serve as reminders. Worked well for fractions lesson on adding fractions.
Luke	Graph paper for operations	X		Much easier to track numbers visually. Last exit ticket, four-question task, got all four correct!
JJ	Formula card	X		Used for multiplying fractions. Leaves cards in class so they are accessible and utilized. Need to create an additional set for homework.

Figure 10.13: Class Sample of What Is Working/What Is Not Working: Class-at-a-Glance Form

DATE	STRATEGY/ ACCOMMODATION	WORKING	NOT WORKING	NOTES
1/15	Formula card for multiplication		X	Not keeping track of formula cards, so not accessing cards for reference.
1/17	Sticky note prompts	X		Sticky note prompts are helping. They were given right in the lesson and are movable to whatever tool she was using (workbook page, homework).
1/20	Paraphrase, rephrase	X		Alexis is using the sticky note prompt with the formula on it, but sometimes still confuses the steps. We paraphrased the steps, adding a lyric to the steps (divide, multiply, subtract, repeat) and had her rephrase using the tune.

Figure 10.14: Student Sample of What Is Working/What Is Not Working Form

If You Have a Co-Teacher or Teacher's Aide

More than ever, schools are realizing that an inclusive setting will best serve the needs of all struggling learners. This means that in a classroom there can be a general education teacher with either a reading or math AIS (academic intervention support) teacher, an ELL support teacher, a special educator, or a teacher's aide. The good news is that struggling learners of all kinds can access core content and curriculum with appropriate supports in a setting alongside their peers.

The way to have this go well is to implement a co-teaching model. There are five co-teaching models (Friend and Cook 1996): one teach/one support, parallel teaching, alternative teaching, station teaching, and team teaching. I'll outline each model, including a definition, benefits, and when you might consider using each.

CO-TEACHING MODEL #1: ONE TEACH/ONE SUPPORT

The one teach/one support model is built upon the idea that one teacher will take the lead role in implementing a whole-class lesson, and one teacher will take the lead role in scaffolding and supporting any learner who struggles. After the whole-class lesson, each practitioner will support students as necessary during the independent practice. Both teachers are equally essential to the teaching and learning and support the room in a collaborative way.

WHEN IMPLEMENTING THIS MODEL	BENEFITS	WHEN TO USE
• Teachers plan together. The teaching point is part of a unit of study, and teachers meet to design the lesson format, timing, tools, and assessment. • Teacher A does the lesson, and Teacher B provides the support during the lesson. Teacher B can use various methods of support and scaffolding, including checking for understanding, using questioning strategies, providing a visual, modifying materials, or providing an additional explanation.	• The power of two instructional leaders • Clear roles • Direct scaffolding of any learner (not just IEP-mandated students) • On-going assessment and documentation more manageable and central	One teach/one support works anytime, but especially when one teacher feels more confident with the curriculum. This model also works well when the teachers alternate roles. This way, students see both teachers as equally important and essential to the teaching and learning.

CO-TEACHING MODEL #2: STATION TEACHING

The station-teaching model works well in classrooms where small-group learning is valued and used. In the station-teaching model, the learning happens in small groups (stations) where each teacher delivers instruction and provides support. There is a lot of movement and mixing of groups in this model.

WHEN IMPLEMENTING THIS MODEL	BENEFITS	WHEN TO USE
• Both Teacher A and Teacher B plan a lesson for a particular station. Each lesson is different but connected under the umbrella of a unit of study. • Each teacher teaches all learners as students rotate through the station.	• Each teacher interacts with all students • Heterogeneous groupings are possible • Group size is reduced • Designated skill and strategy instruction in appropriate, small groups	Station teaching can be used at any point in a unit of study and at any grade level when teachers want to work in a small-group format to teach strategies and skills.

CO-TEACHING MODEL #3: PARALLEL TEACHING

Parallel teaching is all about differentiation and attending to the nuances of teaching and learning. The content of the lesson is the same. However, teachers will adjust pacing, timing, tools used, and mode of assessment to meet the needs of the learners.

WHEN IMPLEMENTING THIS MODEL	BENEFITS	WHEN TO USE
• Teachers plan together, and the teaching point is the same. • Each teacher teaches the lesson to a (small) group. • The content is the same. However, lessons can be differentiated to meet the needs of that group of learners.	• Lower student-teacher ratio • Great student engagement possible • Differentiation of materials, method of instruction, level of current understanding, pacing	Parallel teaching is the perfect model to use when learning needs feel quite varied and one whole-class lesson does not feel like it will meet the needs of all the learners. In this model, teachers can create groups in one of two ways: separating out those who need additional support and modification, or conversely, taking high flyers as the parallel group.

CO-TEACHING MODEL #4: ALTERNATIVE TEACHING

Alternative teaching is just that—delivering alternative instruction. In the alternative model, not only is the delivery different but the teaching point can be different too.

WHEN IMPLEMENTING THIS MODEL	BENEFITS	WHEN TO USE
• Teachers plan together. • Teacher A teaches whole-class lesson to most. • Teacher B teaches a different lesson to a small group where the instruction needs to be greatly differentiated (e.g., students in need of modification of content, or students with mastery needing enrichment).	• High level of differentiation • Opportunity for small-group instruction where the format and content meets the needs of the learners most • Can vary student content within a unit of study	The alternative model can be used in K–8 in any discipline when it is deemed that a small group of learners has a very different need from the rest of the class.

CO-TEACHING MODEL #5: TEAM TEACHING

The team-teaching model of co-teaching is a highly collaborative model of instruction. In this model, the lesson is co-delivered, and each teacher supports learners during the independent practice. Teachers can choose to divide the lesson naturally as they see fit during the lesson, or they can pre-plan the team teaching (which I suggest). For example, Teacher A starts the lesson (the warm-up), Teacher B delivers the teach portion, Teacher A facilitates the active engagement where students try the skill or strategy, and Teacher B clarifies and links the lesson to the independent practice. When the teacher is not teaching, he or she is observing, taking notes, and supporting all learners.

WHEN IMPLEMENTING THIS MODEL	BENEFITS	WHEN TO USE
• Teachers plan together and co-deliver the instruction. • Teachers can alternate parts/jobs but always have an important, specific role (e.g., Teacher A does the warm-up; Teacher B, the teach; Teacher A, the active engagement/try; Teacher B the clarify/link).	• High level of collaboration • Attention to all parts of a lesson • Shared ownership of content and all students	Team teaching works well across grade levels and disciplines in teaching contexts where the co-teacher is often present. If the co-teacher is in your classroom only on Fridays, this model doesn't work as well because finding time to plan can be a struggle.

To help facilitate co-teaching, I suggest using a planner to plan for instruction and support. Figures 10.15 and 10.16 are examples of planners that can be used for the parallel, station, and alternative teaching models. Figures 10.17 and 10.18 are examples of a planner that can be used to plan for the one teach/one support, and team-teaching models.

CO-TEACHING PLANNER FOR PARALLEL, STATION, AND ALTERNATIVE TEACHING MODELS

Unit of Study:				
	TEACHER A	**MATERIALS**	**TEACHER B**	**MATERIALS**
Unit/Lesson				
Specific Teaching Point				
Students				
Checking for Understanding				

Figure 10.15: Co-Teaching Planner for Parallel, Station, and Alternative Teaching Models

Unit of Study: Probability				
	TEACHER A	**MATERIALS**	**TEACHER B**	**MATERIALS**
Unit/Lesson	Unit 5, Lesson 3	Paper cups, worksheet, anchor chart with definitions of equally likely and not equally likely, class anchor chart of results	Unit 5, Lesson 3	Coins, worksheet
Specific Teaching Point	Determine the difference between equally likely and not equally likely		Calculate experimental probability	
Students	Half of class, groups of three		Half of class, groups of three,	
Checking for Understanding	Midpoint questioning, exit tickets		Exit tickets	

Figure 10.16: Sample Co-Teaching Planner, Grade 7, Math, Station-Teaching Model

CO-TEACHING PLANNER FOR ONE TEACH/ONE SUPPORT AND TEAM TEACHING MODELS

Unit of Study:		Lesson:	
STAGE OF THE LESSON	**TEACHER A**	**TEACHER B**	**MATERIALS**
Warm-Up: Engage and connect			
Teach: Demonstrate and model ONE teaching point			
Active Engagement: Let students try			
Clarify: Link to Independent Practice			

Figure 10.17: Co-Teaching Planner One Teach/One Support and Team-Teaching Models

Unit of Study: Narrative Writing		Lesson: Hooking the Reader	
STAGE OF THE LESSON	TEACHER A	TEACHER B	MATERIALS
Warm-Up: Engage and connect	Connects lesson to unit, notes student understanding of hooking reader, tells story of recent conference	Observes students	Previously created anchor chart with dialogue lead Chart paper to compose today's model writing Sticky note prompts
Teach: Demonstrate and model ONE teaching point	Observes students, prompts students to materials	Refers to previously used lead, reminds students of that strategy, demonstrates how to start with setting	
Active Engagement: Let students try	Asks students to notice demo; asks student to "write in the air" to partner showing how they could start their piece with setting	Listens in to *turn and talk*; restates student ideas, supporting their writing in the air; jots key ideas for one student on sticky note, gives to student	
Clarify: Link to independent practice	Asks students who need to clarify to stay in meeting area, reinforces teaching point	Restates teaching point, linking to independent practice	

Figure 10.18: Sample Co-Teaching Planner, Grade 4, Writing, Team-Teaching Model

Final Thoughts

Supporting struggling learners is hard work, but it is work that can bring us great success and joy as educators. When we believe that learners are all different, and that our teaching moves can impact students in profound and powerful ways, then it will be true. I end with some final thoughts on our role as teachers of all children.

This I believe:

- Every child has the right and the capacity to learn. All students are capable, and it is the teaching that needs to change when learning isn't happening.
- Every learner has strengths, and it is upon those strengths that the most growth can occur. We need to be sure that we are living in a way that allows us to capture the strengths and the struggles of each of our students.
- Inclusion is a mindset, not just a place or a method of programming. Therefore, I believe that all learners should be included in my teaching, in my classroom, and in our community.
- The environment in which we learn can either support or impede learners. Environments need to be organized, supportive, appealing, and clutter-free.
- Relationships matter. Students and teachers are their best selves when they connect in positive ways.
- Learners are all different, and, therefore, classrooms, at their core, should be workshops and laboratories. They should be messy and fun and, at best, organized chaos. Learning is differentiated, and students are simultaneously independent and collaborative.

Supporting struggling learners will be at once exhausting, joyful, trying, and rewarding. Harness the power of implementing teaching moves that are geared specifically to our struggling students—to their strengths and to what they need most in this moment to move them forward.

References

Allington, Richard L. 2005. *What Really Matters for Struggling Readers: Designing Research-Based Programs*. 2nd ed. Boston: Allyn & Bacon.

Allington, Richard L., and Rachael E. Gabriel. 2012. "Every Child, Every Day." *Educational Leadership*, March 2012: 10-15.

Anderson, Edward "Chip". 2005. "Strengths-Based Educating: A Concrete Way to Bring Out the Best in Students---and Yourself." *Educational Horizons*, Spring: 180-189. Accessed March/April 2016. http://files.eric.ed.gov/fulltext/EJ685057.pdf.

Beers, Kylene. 2002. *When Kids Can't Read—What Teachers Can Do: A Guide for Teachers 6-12*. Portsmouth, NH: Heinemann.

Benjamin, Arthur. "A Performance of Mathemagic." Filmed February 2005. TED video, 15:14. www.ted.com/arthur_benjamin_does_mathemagic.

Berg, Jessica L., and Joseph Wehby. 2013. "Preteaching Strategies to Improve Student Learning in Content Area Classes." *Intervention in School and Clinic* 49 (1): 14-20. March 15. doi: 10.1177/1053451213480029.

Boushey, Gail, and Joan Moser. 2006. *The Daily Five: Fostering Literacy Independence in the Elementary Grades*. Portland, ME: Stenhouse.

"BrainPOP." Accessed April 1, 2016. www.brainpop.com.

Cain, Susan. "The Power of Introverts." Filmed February 2012. TED video, 19:04. www.ted.com/talks/susan_cain_the_power_of_introverts.

Cambria, Jenna, and John T. Guthrie. 2010. "Motivating and Engaging Students in Reading." *The NERA Journal* 46(1): 16-29.

Center on the Developing Child. 2011. "Executive Function and Self-Regulation." Harvard University. Retrieved May 5, 2016. http://developingchild.harvard.edu/science/key-concepts/executive-function.

Chase, William G., and Herbert A. Simon. 1973. "Perception in Chess." *Cognitive Psychology* 4(1): 55-81.

Clifton, Donald O., Edward Anderson, and Laurie A. Schreiner. 2016. *StrengthsQuest: Discover and Develop Your Strengths in Academics, Career, and Beyond*. Washington, DC: Gallup Organization.

Confucius. "I Hear and I Forget. I See and I Remember. I Do and I Understand." BrainyQuote. Accessed April 2016. www.brainyquote.com/quotes/confucius136802.html.

Conn-Powers, Michael, Alice Frazeur Cross, Elizabeth Krider Traub, and Lois Hutter-Pishgahi. 2006. "The Universal Design of Early Education Moving Forward for All Children." National Association for the Education of Young Children, *Young Children Journal*. Accessed April 1, 2016. http://journal.naeyc.org/btj/200609 /ConnPowersBTJ.pdf.

Cummins, Jim, and Merrill Swain. 1986. *Bilingualism in Education: Aspects of Theory, Research, and Practice*. London: Addison Wesley Longman. doi:10.1177/00224669050 390010301.

Daniels, Harvey, and Nancy Steineke. 2011. *Texts and Lessons for Content Area Reading*. Portsmouth, NH: Heinemann.

Ehri, Linnea C., Louis G. Dreyer, Bert Flugman, and Alan Gross. 2007. "Reading Rescue: An Effective Tutoring Intervention Model for Language Minority Students Who Are Struggling Readers in First Grade." *American Educational Research Journal* 44(2): 414-48.

Eickholdt, Lisa. 2015. *Learning from Classmates: Using Students' Writing as Mentor Texts*. Portsmouth, NH: Heinemann.

Elbow, Peter. 1981. *Writing with Power: Techniques for Mastering the Writing Process*. New York: Oxford University Press.

Fall, Randy, N. Noreen M. Webb, and Naomi Chudowsky. 2000. "Group Discussing and Large-Scale Language Arts Assessment: Effects on Students' Comprehension." *American Educational Research Journal* 37(4): 911-41.

Fearn, Leif, and Nancy Farnan. 2000. *Interactions: Teaching Writing and the Language Arts*. Boston: Houghton Mifflin Company.

Fisher, Douglas, and Nancy Frey. "A Range of Writing Across the Content Areas." Reading Rockets. Accessed July 18, 2016. www.readingrockets.org/article/range -writing-across-content-areas.

Fountas, Irene C., and Gay Su Pinnell. 1996. *Guided Reading: Good First Teaching for All Children*. Portsmouth, NH: Heinemann.

Friend, Marilyn, and Lynne Cook. 1996. *Interactions: Collaboration Skills for School Professionals*. White Plains, NY: Longman.

Gardner, Howard. 1983/2011. *Frames of Mind: The Theory of Multiple Intelligences*. New York: Basic Books.

Gevinson, Tavi. "A Teen Just Trying to Figure It Out." Filmed March 2012. TED video, 7:30. www.ted.com/talks/tavi_gevinson_a_teen_just_trying_to_figure_it_out.

Graham, Steve, and Karen R. Harris. 2005. "Improving the Writing Performance of Young Struggling Writers: Theoretical and Programmatic Research from the Center on Accelerating Student Learning." *The Journal of Special Education* 39(1): 19-33.

Hattie, John. 2009. *Visible Learning: A Synthesis of Over 800 Meta-Analyses Relating to Achievement*. London: Routledge.

_____. 2012. *Visible Learning for Teachers*. New York: Routledge.

Henderson, Anne T., and Karen L. Mapp. 2002. "A New Wave of Evidence: The Impact of School, Family, and Community Connections on Student Achievement." Austin, TX: National Center for Family and Community Connections with Schools.

Howard, Mary. 2009. *RTI from All Sides: What Every Teacher Needs to Know*. Portsmouth, NH: Heinemann.

"Interactive Learning and Reading Activities for Students in Grades PreK-12." Scholastic Teachers. Accessed June 20, 2016. www.scholastic.com/teachers/student-activities.

"Introduction to Surface Area and Volume." Accessed April 2016. www.youtube.com/watch /?v=SJGpKnI-784.

Jenkins, Joseph R., Laurence R. Antil, Susan K. Wayne, and Patricia F. Vadasy. 2003. "How Cooperative Learning Works for Special Education and Remedial Students." *Exceptional Children* 69 (3): 279-292. www.casenex.com/casenex/cecReadings/how CooperativeLearning.pdf.

Khan Academy. Accessed April 2016. www.khanacademy.org.

Lalley, James P., and Robert H. Miller. 2006. "Effects of Pre-Teaching and Re-Teaching on Math Achievement and Academic Self-Concept of Students with Low Achievement in Math." *Education* 126(4): 747-55.

Mason, C., R. Orkwis, and R. Scott. 2005. "Instructional Theories Supporting Universal Design for Learning—Teaching to Individual Learners." In *Universal Design for Learning: A Guide for Teachers and Education Professionals*, Chapter 3, edited by the Council for Exceptional Children. Upper Saddle River, NJ: Merrill Prentice Hall.

Miller, George. 1956. "The Magical Number Seven, Plus or Minus Two: Some Limits on Our Capacity for Processing Information." *The Psychological Review* 63: 81-97.

Minkel, Justin. 2015. "Why I Prefer Pre-Teaching to Remediation for Struggling Students." *Education Week Teacher*. Last modified May 18, 2015. www.edweek.org/tm /articles/2015/05/18/why-i-prefer-pre-teaching-to-remediation-for.html.

Munk, JoAnn H., Gordon S. Gibb, and Paul Caldarella. 2009. "Collaborative Preteaching of Students at Risk for Academic Failure." Accessed April 15, 2016. http://isc.sagepub .com/content/45/3/177.extract.

Paivio, Allan. 1986. *Mental Representations: A Dual Coding Approach*. New York: Oxford University Press.

Palmisano, Samuel J. 2010. "Capitalizing on Complexity: Insights from the Global Chief Executive Officer Study." Somers, NY: IBM Corporation. www.ibm.com/common/ssi /cgi-bin/ssialias?htmlfid=GBE03297USEN.

Reeve, Johnmarshall. 2016. "A Grand Theory of Motivation: Why Not?" *Motivation and Emotion* 40(1): 31-35. doi:10.1007/s11031-015-9538-2.

Rivas, Katheryn. 2010. "100 Incredible & Educational Virtual Tours You Don't Want to Miss." *Online Universities.com* (blog), January 5. www.onlineuniversities.com /blog/2010/01/100-incredible-educational-virtual-tours-you-dont-want-to-miss.

Rose, David H., Anne Meyer, Nicole Strangman, and Gabrielle Rappolt. "Using UDL to Support Every Student's Learning." ASCD: Professional Learning and Community for Educators. Accessed May 19, 2016. www.ascd.org/publications/books/101042 /chapters/Using-UDL-to-Support-Every-Student's-Learning.aspx.

Rosenfeld, Malke. 2017. *Math on the Move*. Portsmouth, NH: Heinemann.

Serravallo, Jennifer. 2012. *Independent Reading Assessment: Teacher's Guide, Grade 3*. New York: Scholastic.

Story, Molly F., James L. Mueller, and Ronald L. Mace. 1998. "The Universal Design File: Designing for People of All Ages and Abilities." Center for Universal Design, North Carolina State University, Raleigh, NC.

Swain, Merrill. 1986. "Communicative Competence: Some Roles of Comprehensible Input and Comprehensible Output in Its Development." In J. Cummins and M. Swain (eds.), *Bilingualism in Education* (116-137). New York: Longman.

Tomlinson, Carol Ann. 2014. *The Differentiated Classroom: Responding to the Needs of All Learners*. 2nd ed. Alexandria, VA: Association for Supervision and Development.

Virtual Field Trips. Accessed June 20, 2016. www.virtualfieldtrips.org.

Vitale-Reilly, Patricia. 2015. *Engaging Every Learner: Classroom Principles, Strategies, and Tools*. Portsmouth, NH: Heinemann.

Vygotsky, L.S. 1978. *Mind in Society: The Development of Higher Psychological Processes*. Cambridge, MA: Harvard University Press.

Wagner, Tony. 2010. *The Global Achievement Gap: Why Even Our Best Schools Don't Teach the New Survival Skills Our Children Need—and What We Can Do About It*. New York: Basic Books.

Make students real partners in their learning with *Engaging Every Learner.*

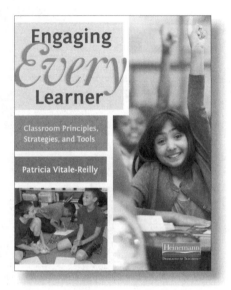

" *Regardless of age, grade level, geographic location, type of school, discipline, or curriculum, a student needs to be engaged in his or her learning in order to excel and succeed.* "

—Patricia Vitale-Reilly

*E*ngagement is cultivated, not taught. Master teacher and education consultant Patricia Vitale-Reilly has a deep understanding of what engagement strategies look like and how to integrate them into classroom practice. In *Engaging Every Learner*, Patricia applies the research on motivation and engagement to strategies and tools that cultivate and sustain student engagement across the school year. She suggests a sequence for implementing the principles of teaching that lead to engaged classrooms, including:

- creating physical, emotional, and cognitive classroom environments for optimal learning

- building meaningful classroom structure through whole class, small group, and independent instruction

- applying the principles of choice to content, process, and product

- connecting students to the world around them through popular culture, technology, and the community.